BEIHEFTE ZUM TÜBINGER ATLAS
DES VORDEREN ORIENTS
herausgegeben im Auftrag des Sonderforschungsbereichs 19
von Wolfgang Röllig

Reihe B
(Geisteswissenschaften)
Nr. 8

Thomas L. Thompson

The Settlement of Sinai and the Negev in the Bronze Age

WIESBADEN 1975
DR. LUDWIG REICHERT VERLAG

The Settlement of Sinai and the Negev in the Bronze Age

by

Thomas L. Thompson

with technical assistance from
Maniragaba Balibutsa

and

Margaret M. Clarkson

WIESBADEN 1975
DR. LUDWIG REICHERT VERLAG

CIP-Kurztitelaufnahme der Deutschen Bibliothek

Thompson, Thomas L.
The settlement of Sinai and the Negev in the Bronze Age / with technical assistance from Maniragaba Balibutsa and Margaret M. Clarkson.
[Diese Arbeit ist im Sonderforschungsbereich 19 Tübingen entstanden.]
(Tübinger Atlas des Vorderen Orients: Beih.: Reihe B, Geisteswiss.; Nr. 8)
ISBN 3-920153-44-8

Diese Arbeit ist im Sonderforschungsbereich 19 Tübingen entstanden und wurde auf seine Veranlassung unter Verwendung der ihm von der Deutschen Forschungsgemeinschaft zur Verfügung gestellten Mittel gedruckt.
Gesamtherstellung: Hessische Druckerei GmbH, Darmstadt
Printed in Germany

To

Dr. John Landgraf

TABLE OF CONTENTS

ABBREVIATIONS

AASOR	Annual of the American Schools of Oriental Research
ADAJ	Annual of the Department of Antiquities of Jordan
AJA	American Journal of Archaeology
BA	Biblical Archaeologist
BASOR	Bulletin of the American Schools of Oriental Research
BIES	Bulletin of the Israel Exploration Society
BZAW	Beiheft zur Zeitschrift für die alt-testamentliche Wissenschaft
ca.	circa
cent.	century
cf.	confer
CRB	Cahièrs de la Revue Biblique
diss.	dissertation
dyn.	dynasty
E	East
EAEHL	Encyclopedia of Archaeological Excavations in the Holy Land
EB	Early Bronze
EEP	Explorations in Eastern Palestine

e.g.	exempli gratia
E.g.	Egyptian grid
EI	Eretz Israel
f.	following
Ğ.	Ğabal
Gl	Glueck
Ḥ.	Ḥorvat
Ḫ.	Ḫirbat
Ha-Aretz	Museum Ha-Aretz Bulletin
Had. Arch.	Hadashot Archaeologiot
HUCA	Hebrew Union College Annual
ibid.	ibidem
IDA	Israel Department of Antiquities
i.e.	id est
IEJ	Israel Exploration Journal
Isr. Gen. Archives	Israel General Archives
JPOS	Journal of the Palestine Oriental Society
km	kilometer
LB	Late Bronze
LB/EI	Late Bronze/Early Iron
m	meter
MB	Middle Bronze
mm	millimeter
N	North
n.	footnote
Ophir	Ophir Expedition to the Negev, University of Tel Aviv
Pal. Mus.	Palestine Museum
PEF	Palestine Exploration Fund

P.g.	Palestine grid
QDAP	Quarterly of the Department of Antiquities of Palestine
RB	Revue Biblique
RM	Ramat Matred
Roth	Rothenberg
S	South
TAVO	Tübinger Atlas des vorderen Orients
vol.	volume
W	West
ZDPV	Zeitschrift des deutschen Palästina-Vereins

INTRODUCTION

The present work is the first of a series of three volumes which will present a collation of the discoveries of Bronze Age remains in the Levant.[1] This volume presents a summary of the sources for three maps dealing with the Bronze Age in Sinai and the Negev which will appear in the Tübingen Atlas of the Near East (Tübinger Atlas des Vorderen Orients: TAVO), which have been collected in the course of my research since the Spring of 1970 undertaken for the Sonderforschungsbereich-19 at the University of Tübingen. The majority of the sites listed here are heretofore unpublished, the information concerning them having been made available to me during the course of three trips to the Near East in 1971/2, 1972/3 and 1974. Although the source of my information for each individual site is given in the "Site List", I wish here to thank the following for their time and the resources which they have made available to me: Mr. R. Cohen, Ms. H. Katzenstein, Mr. A. Kloner, Mr. Y. Landau, Ms. I.Pomerantz, and Dr. D. Urman of the Israel Department of Antiquities in Jerusalem, Dr. E. Oren of the University of Beersheba, and Dr. I. Beit-Arieh, Mr. D. Kozloff, and Prof. Dr. B. Rothenberg of the University of Tel Aviv.

I wish also to take this opportunity to thank Ms. C. Bennett of the British School of Archaeology in Jerusalem and Dr. J. Landgraf of Jerusalem for their advice and hospitality during my visits to Jerusalem. My gratitude is also due to Mr. M. Balibutsa and Ms. M. Clarkson who have given their assistence throughout the production of this Beiheft and the maps

---

[1] The second volume will deal with the Bronze Age remains from Palestine and Transjordan, and volume three will treat the remains from Syria and Lebanon.

which have been prepared for TAVO, and to Dr. M. Kellermann and Dr. M. Wüst for providing me with transcriptions for the Arabic place names. Finally, I wish to thank Professor Dr. A. Kuschke and the Biblical Archaeological Institute of the University of Tübingen for the support which I have received since this work was begun.

The value of this collation is entirely due to the above-acknowledged support; for, while much can be learned from the early explorations of Sinai and the Negev, systematic surveys were first undertaken less than twenty-five years ago, and except for the publications of N. Glueck, B. Rothenberg, and Y. Aharoni, little that is dependable concerning the individual Bronze Age sites in this region can be found in print. The past twenty years have witnessed an intensive exploration of this region, though most of it is still unknown. The results of many of these explorations are still in the process of evaluation, particularly the surveys of I. Beit-Arieh, E. Oren, and B. Rothenberg as well as much of the material from the Survey of the Negev, and the Survey of North Sinai undertaken by the Department of Antiquities. I have used for my collation field notes and written summaries as well as a selective study of some of the pottery and flint artifacts. Other information has been gathered from the National Archives of the Israel Department of Antiquities. The site descriptions presented in the Site List, though dependent on these sources, are nevertheless my own, as is the responsibility for their accuracy.

Since most sites of the Negev and Sinai do not bear names, I have been dependent on grid coordinates and site descriptions for their location. In the case of N. Glueck's published surveys, I have in many cases corrected his published grid coordinates on the basis of the field maps which he used in his survey.[2] In cases where more than one survey has been carried out in the same region, I have been able to collate some sites on the basis of their description. This, however, has not always been possible.

Surface exploration in Sinai and the Negev is also plagued by the lack of adequate criteria for dating pottery and flint artifacts. I have tried to express this uncertainty where applicable in my site description. On one hand there is a problem of adequately distinguishing Chalcolithic-EB I from EB remains in South Sinai. On the other hand, a clear-cut dating for all of the finds from the end of the Bronze Age in South Sinai and the

---

[2] Cf. Th. L. Thompson, "Corrections to the Coordinates of Glueck's Negev Surveys", ZDPV 91, 1975, in press.

Araba is as yet impossible. It is hoped that the designation LB/EI will reflect this uncertainty.[3] Given the uncertainties of pottery classification in Palestine, it is hardly possible to use anything but the most general classifications for finds in Sinai and the Negev during the foreseeable future: Chalcolithic-EB I: ca. 3300-2900 B.C., EB: ca. 2900-2400,[4] EB IV/MB I: 2200-1950, MB II: ca. 1900-1550, LB: ca. 1550-1150, and EI: ca. 1200-1000. In general it is assumed that any given site was occupied during the period or periods assigned to it, but it is not assumed that it was occupied during that entire period; nor can it be assumed that sites given the same classification were contemporary. Moreover, sites which were occupied in successive periods cannot be assumed to have had a continuous occupation. This admittedly puts severe limits on interpretation.

A further limitation on the historical interpretation of the sites here collected is the incompleteness of the exploration. Only the central Negev mountains and the area near Timna in the Araba have been intensively surveyed. Moreover, very few sites have been excavated.

The aim of this work is to present a collection of information that must be taken into consideration in synthesizing the present state of knowledge concerning our period in Sinai and the Negev. The understanding gained by this collation is both fragmentary and uncertain, but nevertheless substantial enough to offer a rudimentary view of the early history of this region. The commentary accompanying the Site List in no way attempts a full-scale treatment of the history of the Bronze Age in Sinai and the Negev. Such a treatment will have to await full publication of the surveys and excavations now in process. Rather, what is offered here is a region by region analysis of the settlement patterns that have become apparent. I will also try to explore the economic basis suggested by these patterns.

---

[3] See on this, now, B. Rothenberg, Timna (London 1972), 105ff, 127ff.

[4] The classification relates this pottery to similar pottery found at Arad; cf., R. Amiran, I. Beit-Arieh, and J. Glass, "The Interrelationship between Arad and Sites in Southern Sinai in the Early Bronze Age II", IEJ 23, 1973, 193-97. That much of the EB pottery in Sinai belongs to EB II is clear; that all of it is to be so dated is still an open question.

PART I

REGIONAL ANALYSIS OF THE ECONOMIC AND GEOGRAPHICAL CONTEXT OF BRONZE AGE REMAINS IN SINAI AND THE NEGEV

1. THE SOUTHERN BORDER OF PALESTINE

The permanently sedentary population of Palestine, throughout its history since as early as the Chalcolithic-EB I period,[5] has followed in its southern limits, with relatively minor variations, the morphological border of Palestine. Throughout this long history the area supporting permanent agricultural settlement reaches its southern limits in the region between the Judeaean hills in the north and the Negev mountains in the south. This border runs through the *Bəẹrševa* Basin and along the *Wādi Ġazza (Naḥal Bəẹrševa)* to the Dead Sea.[6] North of this border, the central mountain range of Judah follows an approximately NNE-SSW direction, forming a relatively flat, broad highland which just south of *Yaṭṭa* drops steeply (450m within approximately 20 kilometers) to the valley floor near *Tall al-Milḥ*. South of this border, a semi-circular region of fold mountains, beginning from the south-west end of the Dead Sea, is formed in a series of five anti-clinal ridges with steep slopes to the SE and SSE and gradual slopes to the NW and NNW. Between these two ranges are the loessial basins of *ʿArād* (ca. 570m) and *Bəẹrševa* (ca. 300m) formed from alluvial sediment.[7]

---

[5] For a convenient treatment of this period, cf., P. R. de Miroschedji, L' Epoque Pré-Urbaine en Palestine, CRB 13, 1971.

[6] Cf. D. H. K. Amiran, "Geomorphology of the Central Negev Highlands", IEJ 1, 1951, 107; also, idem, "Geomorphology", Atlas of Israel, Map II/1.

[7] For more detailed information, cf. S. Ravikovitch, "Soil Map", Israel: 1:250.000, 1970; J. Dan and Z. Raz, "Soil Association Map of Israel: 1: 250.000, 1970.

The rich soil of the *ʿArȧd* and *Bəẹrševa* Basins would offer great agricultural potentialities were it not that the area falls across the border of aridity as well as the morphological border of Palestine. The low-pressure area at the western end of the Mediterranean generally forms its center off the coast of Cyprus resulting in a decreasing amount of rainfall to the south and east. The resulting descrease of rainfall in the southeastern part of Palestine is mitigated only in the higher altitude areas which receive a relatively high amount of rainfall on their northwestern slopes and a proportionately low amount on the southeastern slopes.

The low-lying *Bəẹrševa* Basin received a mean-annual rainfall between 1931 and 1960 of about 150 to 250mm, with the northern part of the basin receiving the greater amount. The *ʿArȧd* Basin received approximately 200mm, with the western portion receiving the greater amount.[8] Temperature, annual evaporation, and solar radiation are relatively high,[9] while humidity and dewfall are low.

The generally accepted limit for the Near East (with dry summers and wet winters), above which unirrigated farming is economically feasible lies between 200 and 300mm of annual rainfall.[10] This suggests that the *Bəẹrševa* Basin lies on the outer extreme of the agriculturally potential regions of Palestine, with the northern part of the Basin at best marginal, and the southern extreme unable to support more than a semi-sedentary subsistence. These characteristics are only partially mitigated by the extremely low gradient (ca. .5% or less) of the *Bəẹrševa* Basin.[11] In sharp contrast to the Central Negev, which we will treat below, the potentially arable fields here receive no supplementary water from run-off unless they lie immediately along the major wādis.

While the modern characteristic of this region, with a climax of

---

[8] Cf. N. Rosenan, "Mean Annual Rainfall", Atlas of Israel, IV/2. Measurements for *Bəẹrševa* itself are reported for the years 1901-1930 and give an average of 192mm of rainfall with a median of 170mm, with dry years registering as low as 76mm: Cf. P. Mayerson, The Ancient Agricultural Regime of Nessana and the Central Negeb (London 1960), 10. From 1920 to 1965 the average rainfall is reported at 195mm, with drought years as low as 42mm: Cf. M. Evenari et alii, the Negev (Oxford 1971), 30.

[9] M. Evenari et alii, The Negev, 34f.

[10] Cf. R. O. Whyte, "The Use of Semi-Arid Lands", in Arid Lands, ed. by E. S. Hills (London 1966), 348.

[11] M. J. Goldschmidt, "Watercourse Gradients", Atlas of Israel, V/2.

Irano-Turanian vegetation,[12] has certainly changed over the years,[13] the basic climate of the arid zones, allowing for some anthropologically important fluctuations, has not basically altered during the last 10.000 years.[14] The basic contemporary agronomic characteristic of a flat, rich, grazing plain, which, however, is capable of supporting at best an uncertain crop of drought-resistent grains, with possible permanent settlement in the northern parts of the region and along the *Wādi Ġazza* can be expected also to be valid for the Bronze Age. The borderline between the settled regions of Palestine and the desert can be expected to shift from north to south within this region following the temporary moderation of climatic conditions on one hand and the technological developments affecting water resources and irrigation on the other.

In each of the periods of the Bronze Age a clear border can be seen separating the permanent agricultural settlements of Palestine from the desert to the south. Through the heart of the *Bəẹrševa* Basin, the border settlements can be traced along the northern arm of the *Wādi Ġazza (Naḥal Bəśor - Naḥal Gərar)*:[15] 0908.01.02, 1008.01, 1108.01.02.03, 1208.01.02, and 1308.02. All the Bronze Age sites as yet reported in the *Bəẹrševa* Basin have been found along the banks of the major wādis or their tributaries, and from the above discussion it may be assumed that the flat plains of the basin itself were incapable of supporting permanent settlement, given the level of technological development during the Bronze Age. Near the western end of the *Bəẹrševa* Basin several sites (1007.01.02.03. 04.05) have been found along the *Naḥal Bəśor (Wādi aš-Šallāla)* with occupation levels from the EB to the LB periods (EB IV/MB I ?). The location of these settlements in the immediate vicinity of *ʿẸn Bəśor (ʿAin Šallāla)* and *ʿẸn Šaruḫen (ʿAin al-Fārʿa)* undoubtedly explains their ability to cope with the aridity of the region.

To the east of the modern city of *Bəẹrševa*, as one enters the *ʿArȧd*

---

[12] M. Zohary, "Vegetation of Israel and the Near East", Atlas of Israel, VI/1.

[13] So, R. O. Whyte, op. cit., 302f.

[14] K. Butzer and C. R. Twindale, "Deserts in the Past", in Arid Lands, 135.

[15] All sites north of the north-south coordinate 060 of the Palestine grid will be published in the "Site List" of the forthcoming TAVO supplement volume: The Bronze Age Settlements of Palestine and Syria, vol. I: South (in preparation).

Basin, a somewhat similar pattern is found along the banks of the *Naḥal Bəẹrševa* and its major tributaries, with, however, somewhat intermittent occupation (1307.01.02.03, 1406.01, 1506.01 and .02). The relatively high-lying *Tẹl ʿArȧd (Tall ʿArād*, 1607.01) represents the eastern extremity of the EB settlements. The one exception to this pattern, 1406.02, with remains from the EB and EB IV/MB I reported, lies on top of a hill on the lower slopes of *Har Dimonȧ*, overlooking *Naḥal Pelet (Wādi Mušāš)*, a tributary of *Naḥal Bəẹrševa*. The EB IV/MB I sites: 1406.03.04.05 will be discussed below. They form the northeasternmost extension of the EB IV/MB I settlements on the northwestern slopes of the Central Negev mountains.

The description of these border settlements which lie along the major wādis of the northern arm of the *Wādi Ġazza* is typical of the Bronze Age settlements of Palestine: small and large tells, in reach of fertile fields and good sources of water, and is in sharp contrast to the typical scattered homestead-like settlement with enclosures, corrals, stone circles, and tumuli, found further to the south in the Central Negev mountains and in Sinai. This line of border settlements forms the southernmost extension of MB II and LB Palestine, beyond which lie the steppe plain of the southern Basin which in the south becomes a sand covered desert before one reaches the Negev mountains, and which in the southeast is cut off by *Har Dimonȧ*.

With the exception of site 1406.02, already mentioned, and, for the EB period, *Tẹl ʿArȧd (Tall ʿArād)*, this line probably forms the southern limit of the village settlements of Palestine during EB and EB IV/MB I as well. Uncertainty arises because of a large group of finds from EB and EB IV/MB I partially reported by Nelson Glueck[16] and the General Archives of the Israel Department of Antiquities (1006.01.02.03.04.05.06.07.08.09 10.11.12), several kilometers south of *Naḥal Bəśor (Wādi Ġazza)*. Two of the EB sites (1006.01.02) lie along the banks of the wādi itself. Though the descriptions of the remains are too cursory to be certain, it seems extremely unlikely that these sites are to be related to the Palestinian settlements, since a distance of 10-15 kilometers separates them from the northern settlements. Moreover, except for the EB sites found along the *Naḥal Bəśor*, their location on and near the sand dunes is anomolous. On the other hand, over 20 kilometers of sand and low-lying desert separate

---

[16] N. Glueck, "Further Explorations in the Negev," BASOR 179, 1965, 21-24.

these sites from the known EB and EB IV/MB I settlements of the central Negev mountains. That these sites may be identified as seasonal settlements related to the grazing of herds could conceiveably be supported by the character of the region which has exceptionally good grazing, but such a theory must depend on a more careful description of the remains than is now available. That they represent a long-term settlement of this region is totally unlikely.

2. The North Sinai Coast

It as as yet impossible to give an adequate analysis of the settlement patterns in the coastal area of south Palestine and North Sinai. During the past fifty years the *Ġazza* region has been disturbed by political disruption, overpopulation through a massive influx of refugees, as well as military occupation, with the result that the archaeological activity in the region has been sporadic and the results available for a regional analysis are extremely fragmentary. Systematic survey of the North Sinai area has only begun,[17] but already the unexpectedly large number of sites discovered in the surveys of E. Oren,[18] when they are sufficiently analyzed and made available, promise to change the entire basis for the discussion of the regional characteristics of the Bronze Age sites in this area.[19] At the present time, however, only the barest skeleton of an analysis can be attempted.

In contrast to the *Bəẹrševa* Basin, the climate along the southern coast of Palestine is strongly mitigated by the influence of the

---

[17] Information on the few sites listed in the Site List for this area has been made accessible to the author primarily through the Israel Department of Antiquities. Most of these sites were found in the course of I. Margovsky's Survey of North Sinai (Cf. I. Margovsky, IEJ 21, 1971, 236; idem, Hadashot Archaeologiot 28-29, 1969, 43-47; idem, Qadmoniot 4, 1971, 18-20). Some sites have also been reported by M. Dothan and A. Berman (Cf. M. Dothan, IEJ 17, 1967, 279f.; idem, 18, 1968, 255f.; idem, EI 9, 1969, 47-59. 135.; Hadashot Archaeologiot 37, 1971, 31-34).

[18] Through personal communication; cf. his preliminary reports: IEJ 23, 1973, 112f.; and idem, "The Overland Route Between Egypt and Canaan in the Early Bronze Age", IEJ 23, 1973, 198-205.

[19] To my great regret, the war of October, 1973, and other commitments of Dr. Oren, have delayed the examination of the survey finds indefinitely, with the result that they cannot be included in the Site List.

Mediterranean Sea. The area between the *wādi Ġazza* and *Naḥal Šiqmā* received an average of between 300 (in the south) and 400mm (in the north) of annual rainfall between 1931 and 1960.[20] The amount of rainfall rapidly diminishes south of the *wādi Ġazza* (e.g., ca. 200-250mm at *Rāfaḥ*) until it reaches an overall average of approximately 150mm along most of the North Sinai coastal strip, an amount which diminishes sharply as one moves inland. Humidity, however, in the *Ġazza* region, is high, particularly during the growing season (approximately 66% from September 1 to April 1), and the dewfall, with approximately 200-250 dewnights (albeit mostly in the summer) adds some 30mm of moisture per year. Though solar radiation is relatively high, the evaporation level is among the lowest in Palestine. Temperatures are moderate and frost is nill. In spite of the fact that the area around *Ġazza* and to the north has predominately a Mediterranean-type vegetation, large areas in the north and most of the area to the south of *Ġazza*, and almost the whole of the North Sinai coast is covered by sand dunes and displays a Saharo-Arabian type vegetation. Along the coast south of *Ġazza* and well to the south of *Rāfaḥ*, however, there are large areas of Brown-Red and Loessial sandy soils with a steppe-like (Irano-Turanian) vegetation. The banks of the *wādi Ġazza* and the *wādi al-ʿArīš*, with large deposits of loessial sediment, also offer a moderate agricultural potential.[21]

The modern city of Ġazza is usually considered historically to be the last major outpost of Palestine before crossing the vast dune-covered desert of North Sinai. The limited archaeological remains available to us today suggest that the border of permanent agricultural settlement during the Bronze Age lies well to the south of the city.[22] Sites 0909.01 (MB II), 0909.02 (EB IV/MB I ?, MB II and LB), 0909.03.04 (EB), and possibly 0909.05 (MB II and LB reported) suggest that at least during the EB,

---

[20] N. Rosenan, loc. cit.

[21] Cf. E. Orni and E. Efrat, Geographie Israels (Jerusalem 1972), 117ff.; Y. Karmon, Israel: A Regional Geography (London 1970), 335ff.; Atlas of Israel, IV 1.2.3 and VI 1; S. Ravikovitch, Soil Map 1:250.000

[22] The possibilities raised by E. Oren's discovery of large numbers of EB and LB sites across most of the North Sinai coast, even though his survey has been carried out only west of *al-ʿArīš*, prevent a too confident acceptance of unexcavated sites along the south Palestinian coast as extensions of the Palestinian agricultural settlements.

MB II, and LB? and possibly during EB IV/MB I the agricultural border of Palestine extended to the banks of the *Wādi Ġazza*. The three small EB tells discovered further to the south along the sea shore (0809.02, 0808.01.02) probably reflect an economy (perhaps fishing) other than agriculture.[23] Two further sites, some 30km NE of *al-ʿArīš*, should also be mentioned as they tend to throw into question any orderly interpretation of the region as a whole. Site 0607.02 is a relatively large tell (ca. 10 dunams) on the edge of sand dunes about 2 1/2km from the coast, with pottery from MB II and LB reported. The other site (0607.01) is on the sand dunes, approximately 1.2km distant and about 2km from the coast. It is a smaller site (ca. 5 dunams) with a great deal of pottery from EB, EB IV/MB I, MB II and MB/LB reported. Were it not that the area between these sites and the *Wādi Ġazza* is so poorly surveyed, one might relate these sites, especially site 0607.01, to the apparently active trade routes suggested by the surveys of Oren and Margovsky along the North Sinai coast.

For the sites in the area west of *Wādi al-ʿArīš*, it is hardly possible to suggest an economic base of agriculture, except perhaps for a few of the sites in the widely scattered oases. Nor do the site descriptions given by Margovsky and suggested by Oren[24] resemble, apart from the large amounts of pottery, what we know of agricultural settlement in the Bronze Age. Military installations, way stations, and campsites seem preferable descriptions. Some of the sites along the sea-shore, such as the very small EB site: 9607.01, could perhaps be related to fishing, but most of the sites are shallow, pottery-strewn areas with few, if any, structures, and far from the sea-coast.[25] Some of the LB sites, such as *Bīr al-ʿAbd*,[26] are most likely military forts or encampments related to some of the New Kingdom campaigns in Palestine. Most of the sites are probably related to trade routes between the Delta and southern Palestine. Both Egyptian and Palestinian wares are common enough to support this,[27] though it does

---

[23] Similarly, the two sites: 0708.01.02, (with MB II and LB sherds) found on the sea shore and described by I. Margovsky as "tells".

[24] E. Oren, IEJ 23, 1973, 198f.

[25] Ibid., 200f.

[26] E. Oren, IEJ 23, 1973, 112f.

[27] Egyptian wares predominate in most cases.

not seem possible to suggest that the trade was controlled either by Egypt or by a hypothetical unified power in south Palestine.

The overwhelming number of Bronze Age sites so far discovered come from the EB and the LB periods. Oren reports that, in at least one area, as many as fifty sites were found in a $10km^2$ region. The sites vary in size from 2 to 15 dunams, and the discovery of "stone tools and patches of burnt soil with remains of cooking installations, e.g., clay ovens and coarse baking bowls with unworked bases, points to a somewhat permanent settlement..."[28] He correctly concludes that such remains hardly testify to "a series of temporary stations or trading posts along a certain road linking Egypt and Canaan."[29] His analogue to the "present-day Bedouin settlements with seasonal and permanent encampments alongside large villages",[30] would be more attractive if large Bronze Age villages in the major arable areas had been found. Could possibly the trade routes have played the role of the present-day large villages -- for the presence of Egyptian and Palestinian remains in these temporary encampments must be explained -- and that, at least during the EB and LB periods (aside from possible LB military sites), the sites reflect two distinct aspects of a single economic phenomenon: those directly related to the trade routes; i.e., temporary encampments and way-stations, and, secondly, those indirectly related to these routes; namely, short-term settlements living in symbiosis with the caravan traffic. Much of this will hopefully be clearer when areas to the north and south of Oren's survey are explored.

A few sites, with finds reported from the EB IV/MB I and MB II periods as well, have been found in this region which are particularly interesting. Sites 9604.02 and .03 are two large sites (30 and 15 dunams respectively) with pottery from both these periods. Approximately 50km to the east a very large (ca. 600 x 600m) site with pottery from EB IV/MB I is reported by Margovsky. Another 12km to the east, there have been reported sites 0205.01 (ca. 10 dunams) with pottery from EB IV/MB I and MB II, and site 0205.02 (ca. 2 1/2 dunams) with EB IV/MB I pottery.[31]

---

[28] Oren, IEJ 23, 1973, 200.

[29] Ibid.

[30] Ibid., and n7.

[31] A third site in this same area, 0205.04, may possibly also have MB II pottery, according to Margovsky's description.

If, of course, the pottery reading is correct, a ready explanation of these quite substantial sites -- especially since the MB II pottery culture is otherwise unknown in Sinai except for a very few mining sites in South Sinai -- is that of way-stations along trade routes. This involves the hypothesis, confirmed for MB II by literary records, that there was indeed a trade route across northern Sinai between Egypt and Palestine during the EB IV/MB I and MB II periods, as well as during the EB and LB periods.

3. The Mountains of the Central Negev and North-Central Sinai

Approximately fifty kilometers southeast of the great sand dune desert of the North Sinai and south Palestinian coastal strip between *al-ᶜArīš* and *Rāfaḥ*, just south of the *Ḥolot Ḥăluṣȧ*, which forms the southern border of the *Bəẹrševa* Basin, a strip of limestone foothills and lowland plains (ca. 10 to 25km wide) rises towards the southeast (elevation: ca. 200-400m).[32] Larger wādis whose ultimate sources are the highlands further to the southeast drain the hill country and cut through the lowland plains in the direction of the Mediterranean, emptying into *Naḥal Bəẹrševa, Naḥal Bəśor, Wādi ᶜAzārīq (Naḥal Niṣȧnȧ)*, and *Wādi al-ᶜArīš*. The hillsides of this lowland strip are covered with a relatively infertile and shallow, gravelly and saline soil. The plains, however, which have their ultimate origin in the highlands, have a 2-3m deposit of loessial alluvial sediment and develop excellent grazing pasturage.

During the EB period, only three sites along the *Naḥal Bəẹrotayim* have been reported in the lowland hill country (0902.06.08 and .13?), and only at the small site 0902.08 were a large number of EB remains found. This region along the *Naḥal Bəẹrotayim* and the *Naḥal Niṣȧnȧ* offer the most favorable ecological region of the hill country, lying ca. 325m above the sea, along one of the major drainage channels coming down from the Negev highlands.

---

[32] For this, and the following, cf. M. Evenari et alii, "Ancient Agriculture in the Negev", Science 133, 1961, 979; E. Orni and E. Efrat, Geographie Israels, 15f.; Y. Karmon, Israel, 275; M. Evenari et alii, The Negev, 43f.; D. Zohary, "Notes on Ancient Agriculture in the Central Negev", IEJ 4, 1954, 17ff.; Y. Kedar, "Water and Soil from the Desert", Geographical Journal 123, 1957, 179-87; D. H. K. Amiran, IEJ 1, 1951, 107.20; L. Shanon, "Rainfall Patterns in the Central Negev Desert", IEJ 17, 1967, 163-84 and the Atlas of Israel.

Even during the EB IV/MB I period, however, when the Central Negev supported the largest population of the Bronze Age, sites are relatively rare and widely scattered in the region of the lower hills. In the extreme northeast, aside from the already mentioned *Ḥ. Mizbāḥ* (1406.02), the narrow strip of foothills to the south of *Naḥal Bəẹrševa* and the *ᶜArād* Basin, is almost entirely devoid of settlement. The three sites along the *Naḥal ᶜĂroᶜẹr* (1406.03.04.05) lie at a height of 375-400m in the valley of *Ḥ. ᶜĂroᶜẹr*. The remains from EB IV/MB I at these sites are insubstantial.[33]

Moving southwestward, there are a number of small EB IV/MB I sites reported at even lower altitudes. Site 1205.01 (ca. 250m) is a lone site situated on the *Naḥal Rəvivim* in the middle of a large rolling plain. Sites 1204.01.02 lie up in the hills (ca. 375 and 325m) overlooking the large alluvial plains, as does site 1003.01 (ca. 350m). Sites 1203.06.13, 1103.01.02, 1003.02.03, and 1002.01 all lie (elevation ca. 250-350m) along or on the slopes of the major wādis as they cut through the plains between the hills. All are small limited sites.[34]

Both the location of the sites and the limited amount of Bronze Age remains found in the hill country make it highly unlikely that any amount of intensive agriculture was carried out at these sites. The rainfall of the area is probably about 100mm or less per year, and, unlike the settlements in the Negev highlands or those along the minor wādis of their northwestern slopes, it is unlikely that major amounts of run-off water could have been efficiently utilized so as to support permanent agricultural settlements. On the other hand, the ecology of the area seems fully adequate to support at least a seasonal occupation of a semi-sedentary population, living off the grazing plains of the lowland plains, occasionally supplemented by the planting of grains after the

---

33 Cf. N. Glueck, "The Fourth Season of Exploration in the Negev", BASOR 142, 1956, 31; idem, "The Fifth Season of Exploration in the Negev", BASOR 145, 1957, 14; idem, "The Negev", BA 22, 1959, 85-87; idem, "Archaeological Exploration of the Negev in 1959", BASOR 159, 1960, 8.

34 The relatively large site, 1304.01, though it lies at an altitude of only 375m, does not fit the pattern of the sites discussed here. Its location on the northwest slopes of the mountain, along the banks of the small tributary *Nahal Maš'abim* resembles, in its location, much more the settlements 6-7km to the south, higher up the slopes of *Har Raḥămā*. Furthermore, it is not clear that the area immediately to the southeast of this site along the lower slopes of *Har Raḥămā* has been adequately surveyed.

occasional major floods.[35] The population on such a marginal basis, given the problems related to water storage, would have had to be quite small.

The large number of sites discovered in and near the flood plains of *Naḥal Niṣànà, Naḥal ᶜĔzuz* and *Naḥal Bəẹrotayim,* several of which are very large and substantial settlements (e.g., 0902.09, 0901.03, 1002.03 .10.12.13), require an entirely different explanation. One of the many possible solutions is to understand the settlement of the flood plains here as the lower limits of the settlement of the lower northwestern slope of the large broken plateau descending from the western end of the *Makteš Ràmon*; i.e., as belonging to the same basic ecological region as the higher lying sites 1001.01-.07, 1000.02.04.05.[36] Certainly the larger sites, especially 0902.09 and 1002.10, reflect a major and perhaps sedentary settlement of this region, and require that this area be considered in connection with the highland settlements.

The archaeological survey of North-Central Sinai has only begun, and it is as yet impossible to speak of "patterns" of settlement. Moreover, due to the lack of dependable data, the climate can only be estimated on the basis of a comparison with the Negev. However, even the relatively cursory surveys of Margovsky and Rothenberg, along and near several of the major roads and paths, give evidence of the settlement of large areas of this region in both the Chalcolithic-EB I and the EB IV/MB I periods. The Chalcolithic-EB I sites (0499.01, 9696.01, 9495.01.02, 9695.01, 9691.01, 9694.01.02, 9493.01.02 and especially 9591.01) are generally small and ephemeral, resembling some of the sites reported by Glueck in the *Bəẹrševa* region,[37] and reported in a few widely scattered areas of the central Negev highlands and the northern section of the *Wādi ᶜAraba*. They possibly represent some of the remains of a still semi-sedentary culture whose economic centers lie rather in the mining regions of South Sinai and the

[35] I doubt that it can be assumed that the EB IV/MB I population had developed a technology sufficient to control the floods on the major plains, as was done during the Roman and Byzantine peiods . See on this, M. Evenari et alii, Negev, 95-119.

[36] An "improvement" of climate cannot be the explanation, since an increase of rainfall would also increase the difficulties of controlling the large flood plains, and a greater frequency in the major floods would be detrimental to any undeveloped agriculture.

[37] Cf. N. Glueck, BA 22, 1959, 85f.; idem, BASOR 159, 1960, 8. 12f; idem, "Further Explorations in the Negev", BASOR 179, 1965, 18. 22-28.

southern *ᶜAraba* and the trade routes along the North Sinai coastal area.

The EB IV/MB I sites, which both Margovsky and Rothenberg report, suggest both a substantial and sedentary population in several areas of North-Central Sinai. On the northwest slopes of *Ǧabal Halāl*, Margovsky reports 11 separate EB IV/MB I sites, two of which (0501.03.09) cover very large areas; they lie along or near the smaller wādis and could be compared with the sites in the Negev highlands. I would suggest a similar interpretation for most of the sites reported by Rothenberg far to the west, which were found along the wādis draining the mountains which lie to the east of Suez. The largest and most substantial sites are 9695.01, 9794.01 and 9591.01. All but the last lie at altitudes of about 600m, and may well reflect a type of mixed agricultural and herding economy similar to what I suggest below for the central Negev highlands. 9591.01, though it is situated at an altitude of only ca. 400m, is near good arable fields in the tributaries of *Wādi as-Sūdr* and within easy distance of several major springs. A few of the smaller sites, on the other hand, (e.g., 9495.01.02, 9493.01.02) are probably better compared with the semi-sedentary sites in the Negev foothills and lowlands.

As mentioned above, the central Negev highlands, forming a morphological and climatic unit with Sinai, consist of a series of parallel anticlines, composed of limestones and cherts, and extend in an approximately NE-SW and, in the western zone, an ENE-WSW direction.[38] The elevation of the mountain range is modest, with a gradual rise to the south of about 600 meters (ca. 420-1035m elevation) over a distance of about 50 kilometers to the southeast end of the *Maḵteš Ramon*, with an average elevation of about 650m. Ecologically important erosive cirques (most important are the *Maḵteš Ramon* and the *Maḵteš Ha-Gadol*) have developed along the crest of the ridges, resulting in a marked climatic change at the upper lip of the cirques. The SE and SSE slopes of the central mountains descend at a rate of 30-45%, forming a steep scarp west of the *ᶜAraba*. Through water and wind erosion, this area has lost most of its soil except in a few wādi beds, where the vegetation supplies a scant winter pasturage. In contrast, the NW and NNW slopes (with an equally advanced erosion), because of their very gradual slope of 6-10%, have developed a trellis-like network of wādis with strips of alluvial loess

---

[38] From *Har Dimona* to *Ǧabal ᶜArīf*.

on the banks of the smaller wādis, and deep loessial plains along the major wādis. The watersheds form large plains.

It is on the northwestern slopes and in the higher hills west and southwest of *Makteš Råmon* that a very large number of EB IV/MB I settlements have been found. The size and type of settlements in this area are quite varied. Most are small homestead-like sites with animal enclosures and from 5 to 15 stone circles (or at times, square house structures), and a small number of tumuli.[39] Others consist of only one or two circles, enclosures, or tumuli. Many of the settlements, however, are very large, covering areas of nearly a kilometer, but still with the same basic pattern of structures.[40]

Aside from a few sites near springs or oases, most of the sites on the northwestern slopes of the ridges are found above or near the smaller wādis; a few are found in the major loessial plains, and a number are found on hill tops and slopes far from the wādis. On *Ramat Maṭred* and in the area to the west and southwest of *Makteš Råmon*, on the other hand, only a few sites are found near arable wādis, and the majority were found along the slopes and gullies of the upper plateau. Not only because of the location of many sites near terraced wādis,[41] but also through the discoveries of grinding stones, sickle blades, and agriculturally related seeds and grains,[42] it is clear that at least some agriculture was practiced in the Central Negev during the EB IV/MB I period. The extent of the agricultural activites of the polulation, however, can only be estimated on the basis of the nature and location of the settlements on one

---

39 The tumuli are only sometimes used for burials; many may have been used for storage or other purposes.

40 . For a more complete description of these remains, cf. the articles of N. Glueck, passim; also, Y. Aharoni, "The Ancient Desert Agriculture of the Negev, Early Beginnings", IEJ 8, 1958, 231-68; idem, "The Ancient Desert Agriculture of the Negev. V; an Israelite Agricultural Settlement at Ramat Maṭred," IEJ 10, 1960, 23-36, 97-111; B. Rothenberg, God's Wilderness (London 1961), 60-63; and, especially, M. Kochavi, "The Excavations at Tell Yeroham", BIES 27, 1963, 284-92; idem, The Settlement of the Negev in the Middle Bronze I Age (Jerusalem dissertation, 1967).

41 Cf., e.g., the drawing in B. Rothenberg, God's Wilderness, 61.

42 See especially Kochavi, but also Glueck, passim (cf. above n40); also Y. Aharoni et alii, "The Ancient Desert Agriculture of the Negev III. Early Beginnings", IEJ 8, 1968, 236. 248.

hand and the ecological capabilities of the region on the other.[43]

The northeasternmost of the EB IV/MB I settlements of the Central Negev on *Har Dimonā* offer a picture of contrasts. There is a group of small settlements (1506.03-.05, 1405.01.02, 1505.01-.06), which lie along the smaller wādis or on small hills between the wādis on the northwestern slopes of the mountain at a height of ca. 375 to 600m. In the high-lying plain of the watershed (ca. 575m) three very large, possibly related, settlements are reported (1505.08-.10). To the southeast, in the hills along the ridge (ca. 500m) before the slope drops sharply to the *wādi ᶜAraba* another group of sites is reported (1504.01-.03.05.07). A few scattered remains were also found further down the slope along a small tributary wādi (1504.10). Southwest of these sites, along the upper southwest slopes of the *Maḵteš Ha-Gādol* (elevation 600-700m), we find a number of sites (1504.08.09, 1404.01-.03.07.10), two of which are quite large and substantial, on the slopes or on top of small hills above the many minor wādis descending from the rim of the cirque. One small site, however, (1404.06), seems to be at least a kilometer from any arable fields. To the west of the cirque, but continuing on the upper northwestern slopes descending from the watershed, are a number of settlements (1303.17.20-.32.35-.39.42.43), two of which are large (1303.27.36). All of these sites lie along or on small hills above the descending wādis. The very large site 1302.03 and the smaller sites 1302.04-.08, to the southeast of the watershed along the *Naḥal Ṣin* (elevation: ca. 300m) on its descent to the *Ṣin* Valley, are quite unusual and are almost certainly to be seen as semi-sedentary in nature and as related to grazing.

The long synclinal plain stretching from *Yəroḥām* to *Sədẹ Boqẹr* is largely devoid of EB IV/MB I remains, except for three rather ephemeral sites (1303.41, 1302.01.02) SSE of *Sədẹ Boqẹr*. As soon as one descends from this plain along the slopes to the northwest, large numbers of EB IV/MB I settlements are found (1404.04.05, 1304.01.03.04, 1303.01-.16.18

[43] This region of the Negev is poor in ground water. The sizeable population suggested by the nearly 400 sites of this region, however, forces us to make the assumption that some widespread means of water storage was practiced, though there is as yet little concrete evidence of this. This problem persists whether one would describe the population as primarily agricultural or as living without an agricultural base. It, however, should probably not be assumed that any substantial amount of this storage water was used for supplementary irrigation.

.19.25, 1203.01-.05.07-.10.15-.36, 1202.02.03) on the slopes of the hills along the smaller wādis. Except for site 1202.01 and the neighboring sites 1202.04-.06 at the southern end of the *Naḥal Bəsor*, the large plain developed by the *Naḥal Boqer* and the *Naḥal Bəśor* saw little settlement during this period.

On the high plateau (ca. 550-650m) of *Ramat Maṭred* further to the southeast, we find a very large number of sites with an entirely different pattern. Most of the sites (1202.11.12.16-.19.21-.23.27-.35.38.39.49-.54 .65.67.71.74, 1102.01-.14, 1101.01.02.06.07.11.12) lie scattered along the hills and gentle slopes of the southeasternly tilted plateau, quite far from possibly arable fields. Many others lie high on the plateau, along the smaller wādis and gullies[44] (1202.24-.26.36.37.40-.48.55-.64.66.69 .70, 1101.03-.05.08-.10, 1101.15-.17, 1201.01-.16), most of which, however, drain towards the southeast into the *Naḥal ʿȦvdat*. Some sites are also to be found in or on the slopes above the large plains of *Naḥal Ṣippŏrim* -- *Naḥal Bəśor* and *Naḥal ʿȦvdat* (1202.07-.10.13-.15.20.67.68, 1101.13.14, 1201.17.18), and only minor settlements are found in the region of *ʿẸn ʿȦvdat* and *ʿẸn Marʿărif* (1202.16.17.26). Very few of the sites in this region can be described as possibly related to agriculture.[45]

Southeast of *Naḥal ʿȦvdat*, the hills rise sharply in the direction of the *Makteš Ramon*.[46] Only a few small sites are reported on the steep upper descent of *Naḥal Ṣin*, which at this point comes down the slope in a northerly direction. Along the small tributary wādis in the long alluvial plain formed by *Naḥal Ṣin* and *Naḥal Niṣȧnȧ* on the northwestern rim of the *Makteš Ramon*, a considerable number of settlements (1300.01-.04, 1200.02-.08, 1299.01, 1199.01.02), with some quite large sites (e.g., 1300.02, 1200.07, and 1199.02), have been found in an area which seems well suited to grazing, and which might also, because of its good soil and high

[44] It is possible that the erosion of the soil from some of these gullies postdates the EB IV/MB I period.

[45] See further, Y. Aharoni, IEJ 10, 1960, 26.

[46] This area is not as yet well surveyed, and no strong assumptions can be made about the relatively sparse settlement on the steeply descending slopes above *Naḥal ʿȦvdat* and along the upper *Naḥal Niṣȧnȧ*. A similar scarcity of sites, however, might also be noticed along the steep descent from *Har Romẹm*.

altitude, support a limited amount of agriculture. On and near the watershed to the west of the cirque, another large group of sites has been reported on *Har Romem* (elevation: ca. 1000m). A few of these sites (1099.02, 1199.03-.06) are small settlements on the upper wādis descending the northwestern slope. Most, however (1099.03-.06, 1199.07-.18), including the very largest (1199.10.18) were found on the high steppe plain of the watershed.

Descending the northwestern slope of *Har Romem*, another large group of sites are found along the banks of the lower, gentler sloping wādis[47] in the direction of *ʿAin al-Qudērat* (1000.01 .03.06-.10). EB IV/MB I remains are also reported along the wādi near *ʿAin al Qudēs* (1099.01) and on the northern ridge above the spring (0900.17.18). Near *ʿAin al-Qudērat* a large number of small settlements has been reported (0900.02.06.07.09-.16), particularly along the *Wādi al-ʿAin* and the *Wādi Umm Ḥāšīm*. Another small group of sites was found on *Ǧebel Quṣēma* between *Wādi al-ʿAin* and *ʿAin Quṣēma* (0900.01.03-.05.08). Scattered EB IV/MB I remains have also been reported further down the slope (elevation ca. 300m) along the *wādi Muwēliḥ* (0801.01.02), about 3-4km northwest of *ʿAin Quṣēma*.

South of the *Maktes̆ Ramon* a number of widely scattered sites (1298 .01.02.03, 1198.01-.03, 1297.01-.05), a few of which can be described as large and substantial settlements (1298.02, 1198.01, 1297.01.03), were found at an altitude of ca. 700-800m along the gentle, easterly sloping wādis and steppe plains, below the steep scarps of the *Maktes̆ Ramon, Har Loṣ, Har Batur,* and *Har S̆agiʾ* and above the steep descent to the *ʿAraba* Valley. The only other signigicant group of sites in the central Negev mountains are the settlements high on the southern slopes of *Ǧabal Muǧārā* near *ʿAin Muǧārā*.

The patterns formed in the location of the EB IV/MB I sites in the central Negev mountains suggest that the settlement of the Negev during this period be interpreted as based on a mixed economy of agriculture and grazing. The many sites along the smaller wādis (particularly: those along the northwestern slopes of *Har Dimona*, the upper slopes of the *Maktes̆ Ha-Gadol*, the descent from the *Yǝroham-Sǝdẹ Boqẹr* plain, the slopes above *ʿAin al-Qudērat*, a few of the sites on the eastern side of *Ramat Maṭred*, and perhaps some of the settlements on the upper northwest slopes of

[47] From ca. 700-500m elevation.

Har Romẹm and the southern slopes descending from Makteš Rắmon) seem best
explained in terms of agriculture. This could also be the case of those
found in the immediate vicinity of springs, though these sites could as
well be understood as related to animal husbandry. Most of the remaining
sites on the other hand, especially those found in the high-lying regions
of Ramat Maṭred, Har Romẹm, the plain of Naḥal Sin and the upper Naḥal
Niṣáná, and the sites along the watersheds, lie in areas where not only is
grazing good, but where there seem to be insurmountable obstacles to any
intensive agriculture.

The suggestion that many of the sites here discussed ought to be:
understood as sedentary agricultural settlements seems necessary, not only
because it seems hardly possible for such a large population (as must be
assumed for such a great number of sites, many of which, e.g., Tẹl Yɘroḥắm,
are both extremely large by Bronze Age standards as well as long-term
settlements) to support large enough herds for subsistence, but also
because of their location. In the immediate vicinity, where most of the
settlements which I would designate as possibly agricultural are situated,
are the major synclinal valleys of Yɘroḥắm-Sɘdẹ Boqẹr and Naḥal Boqẹr-Naḥal
Bɘšor. But these plains, though supporting good grazing lands, are
singularly lacking in intensive settlement. Even the Naḥal ʿÀvdat has a
comparatively limited settlement during this period. When the ecological
contingencies related to primitive agriculture in this region are considered, it might also be suggested that the narrow alluvial plains along
the smaller wādis descending the northwestern slopes of the central mountain range are adequate to support an albeit precarious and marginal
existence for a considerable number of people. It is unlikely, however,
that large flocks could be supported on the natural vegetation of these
same wādis without a considerable agricultural supplement.

These ecological contingencies can be briefly described. Though
there has been widespread deterioration of arable land in the Central Negev
since at least the eighth century as a result of neglect of the necessary
conservation of soils, particularly along the smaller wādis where erosion
has carried large amounts of good soil into the major plains, there are
still large areas in this semi-arid zone which are suitable for agriculture, given a maximum use of the available rainfall.[48] The climate as a

[48] R. O. Whyte, in Arid Lands, 302; G. E. Kirk, "The Negev, or
Southern Desert of Palestine", PEQ 73, 1941, 70; M. Evenari et alii,
Science 133, 1961, 982.

whole ranges between arid and semi-arid. Dependable statistics of mean annual rainfall are available for the Negev highlands only in the areas of *Sədẹ Boqẹr* (76mm), *ᶜÅvdat* (83mm), *Šivṭå* (86mm), *Bīr Asluǧ* (86mm), *ᶜAuǧa* (65mm), and *Mamšit* (80mm).[49] Moreover, rainfall patterns in the Negev are quite varied and there can be sharply divergent rain patterns over very short distances. Estimates based on altitude and vegetation generally range from somewhat less than 90mm for the lower northwestern slopes of the mountains to as high as 150mm on the northern rim of the *Maḵteš Råmon*, and dropping sharply along the south-eastern slopes and the descent to the *Wādi ᶜAraba* to approximately 20-50mm.[50] Similarly, the vegetation ranges between a steppe-like Irano-Turanian vegetation and the Saharo-Arabian vegetation of the desert. That the rainfall occurs primarily in light showers of 3-8mm, and that it falls in the winter time during the growing seasons, and moreover, at a time when, because of lower temperatures and cloud coverage, evaporation is at a minimum, a greater than normal proportion of the rainfall is productive. Mean temperatures, particularly during the growing season, are moderate, while solar radiation is extremely high. Dewfall is also high (*ᶜÅvdat*: 33mm) as are the number of dewnights (*ᶜÅvdat*: 195 per year) on the western slopes of the mountains. However, unlike the *Ġazza* region, they occur principally in the months of September, October, and November.[51] Of far more importance to the survival of agriculture in this region, given the low annual rainfall (The area is totally incapable of supporting dry-land farming) is the amount of water reaching the arable fields, and how this water is controlled. L. Shanon suggests the following distribution of water for plant use in the different ecological regions of the Central Negev: along the rocky slopes, ca.

---

[49] Cf. M. Evenari et alii, ibid.; idem, Negev, 30; P. Mayerson, Ancient Agricultural Regime, 10.

[50] Y. Kedar, Geographical Journal 123, 1957, 180; L. Shanon et alii, "Rainfall Patterns in the Central Negev Desert", IEJ 17, 1967, 163; Y. Kedar, "Ancient Agriculture in the Negev", IEJ 7, 1957, 180, suggests what seems an unlikely 200mm rainfall at elevations above 900m.

[51] D. Ashbel, "On the Importance of Dew in Palestine", JPOS 16, 1936, 316-21; idem, "Frequency and Distribution of Dew in Palestine", The Geographical Review 39, 1949, 291-97; M. Evenari et alii, Negev, 34-36. The effect of dew on plant growth should not be underestimated; for though the total effect on plants in semi-arid climates is not well understood, the summer vegetable crop from the high dew areas of the *Ġazza* strip and the *Hebron* hills is totally dependent on dew formation.

10-60mm; in the loessial plains, 20-50mm; in the gravelly wādis: 60-100mm, and in the loessial wādis: 400-600mm![52] Successful cultivation is possible in the loessial wādis which receive a considerable supplement of water in the form of run-off from the higher lying slopes.[53] Irrigation by flood waters, however, must take active steps to protect the agricultural fields from flood damage. Control of the larger flood plains, wtth the development of dams, sluices, and run-off channels, necessary to control the large flood plains, does not seem to have been developed before the Iron Age. The terracing of the smaller wādis into a series of level plots, on the other hand, requires little expertise, and effectively utilizes the water derived from the slopes as well as prevents erosion.[54]

Primitive cultivation of this sort would probably be confined to the region where Irano-Turanian vegetation is found, in the strips and patches of arable land formed by the smaller wādi beds. Historically, the main crops that have been produced in this region have been grains and legumes, particularly barley, wheat and lentils, but also olives, almonds, dates, figs, apples, grapes, and pomegranates have been reportedly grown in these wādis by the nineteenth and twentieth century Arab farmers.[55]

In concluding this section, it should be pointed out that, although the economy of the EB IV/MB.I settlements seems to have been based on both agricultural and animal husbandry, this conclusion does not require the interpretation that the population was divided between farmers and shepherds; for the differences in the settlement patterns that have been noticed have not been so much in the types of settlement -- indeed, a great homogeneity is apparent -- but in the ecological regions in which the settlements have been found. It seems quite possible that many of the settlements in both types of regions were quite transitory and perhaps even

---

[52] L. Shanon, IEJ 17, 1967, 165; cf. also Y. Kedar, IEJ 7, 1957, 181; idem, Geographical Journal 123, 1957, 180; Y. Aharoni et alii, IEJ 8, 1958, 231-68; M. Evenari et alii, The Negev, passim.

[53] D. Zohary, "Notes on Ancient Agriculture in the Central Negev", IEJ 4, 1954, 19-22. The ratio of catchement areas to cultivated fields varies from 17-30:1 (M. Evenari et alii, Science 123, 1961, 985).

[54] See the excellent and very detailed discussions of this in M. Evenari et alii, Negev, 95-119 and P. Mayerson, Ancient Agricultural Regime, 23-36.

[55] D. Zohary, IEJ 4, 1954, 24.

seasonal, and that the economy of the population as a whole has a mixed base, the settlements living off both their farms and their herds. The Arab population of this area, at least until 1948,[56] living as they have on the basis of a split agricultural-herding economy, might provide a useful analogy; for many of the fields which they cultivated were in the area which we have suggested to have been an agricultural area during the EB IV/MB I period.

4. The Mining Industries of the Wādi ʿAraba and South Sinai

Apart from a few of the larger oases and some patch cultivation in limited areas, the desert region of the *wādi ʿAraba* and southern Sinai seems devoid of settlements based on agriculture. Nevertheless, from as early as the Chalcolithic-EB I period, large numbers of permanent and semi-sedentary settlements were supported directly or indirectly by an extensive copper industry.[57] On the basis of the surveys and excavations so far undertaken, the main periods of exploitation of the copper deposits of the area were during the Chalcolithic-EB I in both Sinai and the *ʿAraba* and the Ramesside LB/EI period in the southern *ʿAraba*, though considerable remains related to metallurgical activities from the EB period in southern Sinai and the EB IV/MB I period in the *ʿAraba* have also been reported. There was also a limited interest in both the turquoise and copper of southern Sinai during the MB II and LB periods.

During the Chalcolithic-EB I and EB periods, the copper industry seems to have been developed by the indigenous population. During the earlier period, there seems to have been a semi-sedentary settlement of the entire south, in small groups along and near the major wādis, whose livelihood was most likely gained through animal husbandry, but whose

---

[56] See on this, the book of E. Marx, Bedouin of the Negev (Manchester 1967), especially 3-68, 81-100. It would be a mistake to consider the post-1948 population for the analogy, not only because the population has been greatly reduced and large numbers of the remainder are partially confined to reservations near *Dimoná*, but also because the artificial effect of the rising demand for meat in Israel has tended to greatly increase the size of the herds and has led to a disproportionate dependence on flocks as a cash producing product, and a consequent neglect of an agriculture which cannot compete in a national market.

[57] See now, the extensive report made by B. Rothenberg, Timna (London 1972).

central and perhaps essential industry was related to the mining of copper. The material remains of the Sinai settlements at this period reflect extensive contact with Egypt (cf. sites 9788.03, 9883.01.03, 9982.02, 0578 .10). In the EB sites, on the other hand, much of the pottery may possibly have been imported from Palestine,[58] though the nature of many of the settlements suggests that the population working and living near the mines was indigenous to the area.

The mining activity of the Chalcolithic-EB I settlements in the *ʿAraba* extended from the region *Yǒtvátá* to the *Gulf of Aqaba*, along the western slopes of *Har Šaḥărur* (1592.04.07?) and south and southwestwards along the western side of the *ʿAraba* (1490.12.13.16.24, 1591.04, 1488.02?). Copper exploitation was also carried out along the steep scarp to the west of the *ʿAraba* (1491.14: copper mine), and in the mountains above the *ʿAraba* (1491 .06). In and along the *ʿAraba* a large number of sites with dwelling structures and corrals for flocks have been found in the area of the copper works (1592.01.08.09, 1491.03, 1591.01-.06, 1490.03?.07?.10?.15.18, 1489.06.07?, 1488.05, 1386.01?, 1486.02?). On top of the hills to the west there are many Chalcolithic-EB I dwelling sites situated at an elevation of ca. 400-600m in the area of the *Biqʿat ʿUvdá* and the *Biqʿat Sayárim* (1493.01-.05, 1492.01-.07, 1391.01.02.05), and also in the mountains (elevation: 700-800m) further to the south (1491.02.04-.06, 1390.01 -.04, 1389.01-.05, 1288.02.03, 1388.01-.06). Similar settlements of apparently semi-sedentary shepherds are found far to the west of the *ʿAraba* rift, along and near the wādis (elevation, ca. 700-800m) of the northern slopes of the Sinai mountains (0588.01, 0788.01.02, 0889.01-.04, 0990.01.02, 1090.01, 1089.01-.07, 1189.01-.04). They are also found along the *Wādi Ǧidda* (0587.01, 0586.01-.04, 0685.01-.04, 0684.01), reaching deep into the Sinai mountains. The settlements along the northern slopes of the Sinai mountains may perhaps have extended across the entire peninsula to the western edge of the highlands (cf. 9788.01-.04, 9888.01, 9887.02. .04.05, 9786.01, 9886.01.02, 0085.01.02), and the metallurgical remains at site 9788.03 suggest that these people were at least partially engaged in the mining industry.[59]

---

[58] R. Amiran, IEJ 23, 1973, 193-97.

[59] It should be remembered that the survey of Sinai is still fragmentary, and it is to be taken for granted that the first sites found in the areas which have been less intensively surveyed will understandably be those that are situated along the major wādis and near existing roads.

South of *Ǧabal at-Tīḫ*, a considerable number of sites are reported in the lower hills east of the Sinai massif (0084.01, 9983.01, 9882.01, 9982.04, 0182.01, 9881.01, 0181.01, 9980.01, 9979.01, 0177.01, 0277.01), and especially along the *Wādi aš-Šēh* and *Wādi Firān* (9879.01.02, 9980.02, 0080.01.02, 0179.01-.04, 0279.01.02), with possibly Egyptian related turquoise and copper mining at sites 9883.01 and 9982.02. A similarly extensive settlement east of the Sinai massif is also reported (1086.01, 0683.07-.09, 0682.01-.03, 0782.01-.03, 0882.01, 0982.01.02, 0983.01, 1083.01, 1082.01, 0580.01, 0681.01-.06, 0780.01-.03, 0779.01-.03, 0879.01, 0880.01.02, 0981.01), some of which, however, were found high in the mountains (ca. 1400m), e.g., 0683.01-.06. Copper mines and metallurgical sites have been found to the south (especially, 0676.01, 0776.01, 1076.01, 0873.01).

The most intensive mining in Sinai seems to have been carried out in the mountains immediately north of the Sinai massif, though the activities in this region during the Chalcolithic-EB I period (0480.01-.03, 0379.01.02, 0479.01.02.04, 0579.01, 0578.06.08.10, 0678.02-.05) was very moderate compared to the very impressive settlement of the area during the EB period, particularly near *Šēḫ Muḥsin* (0478.02) and *Šēḫ Nabī Ṣāliḥ* (0578.03): cf., especially 0479.01-.05, 0579.05-.12, 0478.01-.03, 0578.01-.05.07.09-.13, 0678.01.02.04.[60] The excavations carried out by Dr. I. Beit-Arieh seem to indicate that the settlement of the area was a relatively permanent non-agricultural settlement, probably indigenous to Sinai with close contacts to Palestine, and based largely on animal husbandry. It is probably in the context of these excavations that the number of widely scattered sites reported from the EB period in Sinai and the Central Negev mountains should be understood.

The copper industry of the EB IV/MB I period is still largely enigmatic. The EB IV/MB I settlement of this region seems hardly extensive enough to understand it as fully indigenous. The mines at this period may possibly have been exploited by the populations of the Central Negev highlands and North-Central Sinai.

While the locations of sites 1600.01 and 1800.01 in the northern *ʿAraba* were obviously chosen because of the nearby springs, and are probably to be understood as related to the grazing of flocks, a large

---

[60] The most important mines and metallurgical sites are 0578.10-.12.

copper smelting site has been found further to the east at *Fēnān* (1900.01). The area is so poorly surveyed, however, that it is difficult to understand the extent and nature of the settlements here. In the southern *ʿAraba*, however, there seem to be sufficient remains to suppose a considerable metallurgical activity, not only because of the mines (1491. 18.19) and processing settlements (1491.06?, 1490.22, 1488.03?), but also because, like the mining industry of the earlier periods, the EB IV/MB I copper working sites were supported by a considerable, at least temporary settlement of the area (1493.01.02.05.06, 1492.03.04.08, 1491.01-.03, 1490.03.20 .21, 1389.05, 1489.01.05, 1387.01). The situation in southern Sinai during this period is much less clear. Little, if any (9983.03?), remains of a metallurgical sort which can be dated to this period have been found, and the widely scattered EB IV/MB I sites of southern Sinai (9788.03, 9888 .01, 9887.01.03-.05, 9987.01, 9786.01, 9886.01.03, 9986.01.02, 9983.03, 9982.04) are perhaps best understood independent of the copper industry, and as the southern extension of the population settled across North Central Sinai and the Central Negev.

The few MB II and LB sites of South Sinai (1489.01?, 9883.01.02, 9983.01-.03, 9982.01-.04, 9981.01, 9979.01, 0179.03.04) are clearly related to the Middle and New Kingdom exploitation of the turquoise (9883.02, 9982.04, 9981.01) and copper mines (9883.01, 9983.03, 9982.01.02) of southeastern Sinai near *Bīr Naṣb* and *Sārābit al-Ḫādim*, with the local, apparently non-sedentary population supplying part of the labor force. The Ramesside exploitation of the mines in the southern *ʿAraba*, on the other hand, was very extensive and the existence of large amounts of local ware at the sites, and the widespread settlement of the area suggest that the mines were worked by local labor under the control of the Egyptian colonial power.[61]

---

[61] Though the absolute chronology of the sites in the southern *ʿAraba* is clearly established through excavation, the dating of "Negev-style" pottery in general (Cf. B. Rothenberg, Timna, 181-83) still seems to be a problem. Admittedly, Glueck's 10th. to 8th. century dating of the "Negev" pottery from the northern Negev is hardly firm; nevertheless, Rothenberg's raising of this chronology to the LB period does not seem entirely justified. Glueck also reports much Iron II pottery at his sites. Moreover, Parr's dating of related pottery in NW Saudi Arabia to the LB and Iron Age is not much firmer than Glueck's dating, and must also be understood in the context of "Edomite" ware, as, for instance, found at *Buṣēra*, much of which is apparently to be dated no earlier than the end of Iron I and probably to Iron II. Whether Rothenberg's LB/EI dating can be applied to sites elsewhere than the southern *ʿAraba* is still a moot question. Furthermore, while Rothenberg describes this pottery as not originating at *Timnáʿ*,

The LB/EI settlements of the southern *ᶜAraba* seem self-enclosed and almost solely related to the exploitation of the mines along the western rim of the *ᶜAraba*. Most of the sites where direct evidence for mining and metal working was found lie on the western side of the *ᶜAraba* in and around the lower hills of the high western scarp (1592.07, 1491.07-.09 .11.12.14.15.18-.24, 1490.01.04-.06.08.09.11.13?.17.19.23?.24, 1489.03.04, 1488.02?.04, 1387.01). Closely associated with these sites are a number of probably domestic supporting settlements (1592.03.05?.06.08?, 1491.03 .10.13.16.17, 1591.02, 1490.05.07, 1489.01?.02, 1388.07, 1488.01), some of which suggest an indigenous population. Site 1491.06 shows that metallurgical activity was also carried out on top of the ridge above the *ᶜAraba*. The neighboring sites (1493.01?.02?.03?, 1492.02?.03.04.07?, 1391.05?), as well as sites 1590.01.02 in the *ᶜAraba*, however, probably reflect, on the other hand, some indigenous settlement which was only marginally related to the metal industry.

The question of routes connecting the mining regions with Egypt and Palestine is particularly awkward to discuss on the basis of archaeological remains. That such roads existed is unquestionable. That they generally followed the routes of the major wadis is no more than common sense, given the topography of Sinai and the Negev. That there should be archaeological remains of this travel, giving us the possibility of reconstructing these routes in the form of permanent or even temporary way stations along a trade route, as we find along the North Sinai coast, however, is hardly to be expected. Beyond the suggestion that such obvious roads as the *Wādi aš-Šēḫ* -- *Wādi Firān* route to Suez, or the *ᶜAraba* north to Palestine, were used, one is lost in speculation, since all major wādis eventually reach the perimeters of southern Sinai. The location of many Chalcolithic-EB I non-metallurgical sites on or near the major wādis is, indeed, self explanatory, given the nature of the climate and the location of the only available sources of grazing land and water on which the

---

(Footnote [61] continued from page 27)
there seems no clear reason to connect these mining sites with the sedentary settlements near *Makteš Ramon*. (See, on the other hand, 1000.02.05 .07.09 and 0995.01, as well as 1600.01.02). The location of the smelting camp 229A (!1491.06) is not unusual (as implied by Rothenberg, Timna, 181f.) for reason of lying on a road leading northwards from the *Timnaᶜ* mines in the south. If it is to be understood to be unusual at all it is because it, along with several LB/EI settlements, lies in the hills above and partially cut off from the k n o w n LB/EI mines by the steep scarp of *Har Berek*.

population of these settlements was dependent. The routes used by the Egyptians during the Middle and New Kingdoms, or in fact during the Ramesside LB/EI period, do not seem to have supported a sedentary settlement to and from the mines. Nor, as we have argued above is there any evidence of a route connecting the sites of the *Timnāʿ* region with the north.

5. SUMMARY

The southern border of the village agriculture of Palestine during the Bronze Age lies along the northern arm of the *Wādi Ġazza* through the center of the *Bəʾerševa* and *ʿĀrad* Basins. Along the coast this border extends at least as far as the banks of the *Wādi Ġazza*. During the Chalcolithic-EB I period, there was a trade route between Egypt and Palestine across the North Sinai coastal region. There is evidence of a very widespread semi-sedentary occupation throughout most of Sinai during this period. In the south of Sinai as well as in the southern *ʿAraba*, these settlements were partially supported by the mining of copper. The evidence from the EB period in Sinai and the Negev is fragmentary. There was an active trade route across North Sinai with an extensive semi-sedentary population living in symbiosis with it. Copper mining was carried out in the south of Sinai, but the extent of this is as yet unclear. A number of sites in Sinai and the central and northern Negev seem to reflect a semi-sedentary occupation. The largest number and best known of the Bronze Age sites of the Negev belong to the EB IV/MB I period. There may have been a trade route across the northern coast of Sinai at this time. While the highlands of the Central Negev and North-Central Sinai saw an intensive sedentary occupation based on a mixed economy of run-off agriculture in the smaller wādis of the northwestern slopes and animal husbandry in the major plains and along the slopes of the upper hills, the lower hill country and areas of Central Sinai seem to have been occupied by related, but non-agricultural settlements. Copper mining was carried out in the *ʿAraba*. Little has been found from the MB II period in Sinai and the Negev. A few sites along the North Sinai coast may reflect caravan trade. There are also Egyptian copper and turquoise mines from the Middle Kingdom. The Late Bronze Age coastal route across North Sinai is well established and was supported by way stations and military installations. A few copper and turquoise mines were exploited during the New Kingdom in southern Sinai, and the copper mines of the southern *ʿAraba* were intensively worked during the Ramesside period. The existence of trade routes is particularly difficult to establish archaeologically, and only the North Sinai route between Egypt and the coast of Palestine is certain.

Tübingen, September, 1974

ZUSAMMENFASSUNG

Die Südgrenze einer von Dörfern aus betriebenen Landwirtschaft in Palästina verläuft während der Bronzezeit entlang dem Nordarm des *Wādi Ġazza* durch das Zentrum des *Bəęrševa*- und *ᶜĀrad*-Beckens. An der Küste erstreckt sich diese Grenze zumindest bis zu den Ufern des *Wādi Ġazza*.

Während des Chalcolithicums/Frühbronze I gab es eine Handelsstraße zwischen Ägypten und Palästina durch das Küstengebiet des Nordsinai. Es gibt Zeugnisse einer sehr weitverbreiteten halbseßhaften Besiedlung fast im ganzen Sinai während dieser Zeit. Im Südsinai ebenso wie in der südlichen *ᶜAraba* wurden diese Siedlungen teilweise durch Kupferbergbau unterstützt.

Zeugnisse aus der Frühbronzezeit sind im Sinai und Negev fragmentarisch. Es gab eine belebte Handelsstraße durch den Nordsinai mit einer umfangreiche halbseßhaften Bevölkerung, die von dieser Straße profitierte. Kupferbergbau wurde im Südsinai ausgeübt, seine Ausbreitung ist jedoch noch ungeklärt. Einige Ortslagen im Sinai und dem zentralen und nördlichen Negev scheinen eine halbseßhafte Bevölkerung wiederzuspiegeln.

Die meisten und bekanntesten bronzezeitlichen Siedlungen des Negev gehören zur EB IV/MB I Zeit. Möglicherweise gab es eine Handelsstraße durch das nördliche Küstengebiet des Sinai zu dieser Zeit. Während das Bergland des Zentralnegev und nördlichen Zentralsinai eine intensive seßhafte Besiedlung aufwiesen, die auf der Basis einer Bewässerungskultur in den kleineren Wādis der Nordwesthängen und Tierzucht auf den größeren Ebenen und an den höheren Hängen der Berge existierten, scheinen die Niederungen und Gebiete des Zentralnegev von vergleichbaren, aber nicht landwirtschaftlichen Siedlungen besiedelt gewesen zu sein. Kupferbergbau wurde in der *ᶜAraba* ausgeübt.

Funde aus der MB II-Zeit sind selten im Sinai und Negev. Einige wenige Siedlungen an der Nordküste Sinais könnten auf Karawanenhandel hinweisen. Es gab auch ägyptische Kupfer- und Türkisminen des Mittleren Reiches.

Die spätbronzezeitliche Küstenstraße durch den Nordsinai ist gut nachweisbar und wurde durch Wegstationen und militärische Einrichtungen gesichert. Einige Kupfer- und Türkisminen wurden während der Zeit des neuen Königreichs im südlichen Sinai ausgebeutet, und in den Kupferminen der südlichen ᶜ*Araba* wurde während der Ramassidenzeit intensiv gearbeitet.

Die Existenz von Handelsstraßen überhaupt ist teilweise archaeologisch schwer nachzuweisen, und nur der Verlauf der Nordsinairoute zwischen Ägypten und der Küste Palästinas ist gewiß nachweisbar.

PART II

SITE LIST

9607.01[*] P.g. 966.071

Name: *Katīb al-Qals.*

Description: EB remains found near *Bīr al-Qals.*

¶ Dothan, EI 9, 1969, 55; Isr. Gen. Archives: IDA.

9805.01 P.g. 98120.05240

Name: None.

Description: Small mound (ca. 40 x 20m) near coast with Egyptian pottery from 18th-20th dyn. (LB/EI).

¶ Margovsky, Survey of North Sinai: IDA.

---

[*] The following list is ordered according to the map coordinates of the Palestine military grid. Following a division of the map into 10km squares, the sites are listed beginning from the West and moving eastwards descending in 10km steps from North to South. The first two numbers represent the 10km coordinate on the East-West grid; the second two, the 10km coordinate on the North-South grid. Within each 10km square the sites are arranged by kilometer in the same order. The last two numbers given represent the order of the site within this 10km square. Sites that lie within the same 1km square are listed successively without regard to their geographic order.

The names of sites and wadis along which sites have been found are listed alphabetically at the back of the volume with references to the list given here.

The bibliography given with each site here provides the sources for the information given in the site list. Particularly since we limited our list to Bronze Age remains only, no effort has been made to make the bibliographical information complete. General bibliography for Sinai and the Negev are found at the back of this study.

9805.02 P.g. 98820.05080

Name: None.

Description: Large site (ca. 10 dunams) in marshy area near coast with some, possibly LB pottery.

¶ Margovsky, Survey of North Sinai: IDA.

0105.01 P.g. 01680.05590

Name: None.

Description: Very large area on sand dunes (ca. 600 x 600m) about 2 1/2km from coast with pottery from EB I (generally Egyptian), EB IV/MB I, and possibly LB.

¶ Margovsky, Survey of North Sinai; Survey of Israel Archives: IDA.

0205.01 P.g. 02650.05825

Name: None.

Description: Large mound (ca. 10 dunams) on sand dunes ca. 1 1/2km from coast with scattered remains and pottery from Chalcolithic-EB I, EB IV/MB I and MB II.

¶ Margovsky, Survey of North Sinai: IDA.

0205.02 P.g. 0272.0582

Name: None.

Description: Mound (ca. 50 x 50m) on sand dunes ca. 1 1/2km from coast with scattered remains and pottery from Chalcolithic-EB I and EB IV/MB I.

¶ Margovsky, Survey of North Sinai: IDA.

0205.03 P.g. 02890.05860

Name: None.

Description: Mound on sand dunes ca. 1km from coast with pottery from EB I - mostly Egyptian in origin.

¶ Margovsky, Survey of North Sinai: IDA.

0205.04 P.g. 0251.0576

Name: None.

Description: Mound on sand dunes (ca. 40 x 40m) about 2km from coast with possibly MB II pottery.

¶ Margovsky, Survey of North Sinai: IDA.

0205.05 P.g. 02680.05720

Name: None.

Description: EB I sherds found (mostly Egyptian) on top of mound in sand dunes ca. 3km from the coast.

¶ Margovsky, Survey of North Sinai: IDA.

1205.01 P.g. 120.052

Name: None.

Description: Scattered remains on the banks of the *Naḥal Rəvivim (Wādi ʿUslūǧ)*. Pottery from EB IV/MB I.

¶ Isr. Gen. Archives: IDA.

1405.01 P.g. 1442.0573

Name: None.

Description: EB IV/MB I settlement with stone circles between *Naḥal Seḵer (Wādi al-Mušāš)* and *Naḥal Yitnån (Wādi ʿArʿara)*.

¶ Survey of the Negev: IDA.

1405.02 P.g. 1448.0575

Name: *Ḥ. Nåzir.*

Description: Small EB IV/MB I settlement (ca. 20 x 20m) with tumuli between *Naḥal Seḵer (Wādi al-Mušāš)* and *Naḥal Yitnån (Wādi ʿArʿara)*. Several wells in area.

¶ Survey of Negev: IDA.

1505.01 P.g. 15115.05890

Name: Gl 273.

Description: Settlement on small hill ca. 1 1/2km NW of *Naḥal ʿĂroʿẹr (Wādi ʿArʿara)* with much EB IV/MB I pottery.

¶ Glueck, BASOR 142, 1956, 18.31; Survey of the Negev: IDA.

1505.02 P.g. 1520.0588

Name: None.

Description: EB IV/MB I settlement with stone circles ca. 1 1/4km N of *Naḥal Mirbåṣ (Wādi ʿArʿara)*.

¶ Survey of Negev: IDA.

1505.03 P.g. 152.057

Name: None.

Description: Stone wall near *Naḥal Mirbåṣ (Wādi ʿArʿara)*; much surface pottery from EB IV/MB I.

¶ Aharoni et alii, IEJ 8, 1958, 237.

1505.04 P.g. 1528.0560

Name: None.

Description: EB IV/MB I settlement with stone circles in hills ca. 1km SW of *Naḥal Mirbåṣ (Wādi ʿArʿara)*.

¶ Survey of Negev: IDA.

1505.05 P.g. 1525.0550

Name: None.

Description: EB IV/MB I settlement with stone circles in hills ca. 1/2km SE of *Borot Dimonå*.

¶ Survey of Israel: IDA.

1505.06 P.g. 1517.0542

Name: None.

Description: EB IV/MB I remains with tumuli in hills ca. 1 1/2km NW of *Dimonå*.

¶ Survey of Negev: IDA.

1505.07 P.g. 155.054

Name: None.

Description: Burials with EB IV/MB I pottery on surface in hills ca. 1 1/2km NE of *Dimonå*.

¶ Isr. Gen. Archives: IDA.

1505.08 P.g. 1542.0530

Name: Gl 311b, *Dimonȧ - Rugm al-Balawī*.

Description: Very large EB IV/MB I settlement ca. 1/2km NE of *Dimonȧ*.

¶ Glueck, BASOR 145, 1957, 14; Survey of Negev: IDA.

1505.09 P.g. 15385.05285

Name: Gl 311, *Dimonȧ - Rugm al-Balawī*.

Description: Very large EB IV/MB I settlement on E edge of *Dimonȧ*.

¶ Glueck, BASOR 145, 1957, 14; Survey of Negev: IDA.

1505.10 P.g. 1541.0527

Name: Gl 311a, *Dimonȧ - Rugm al-Balawī*.

Description: Very large EB IV/MB I settlement ca. 1/4km E of *Dimonȧ*.

¶ Glueck, BASOR 145, 1957, 14; Survey of Negev: IDA.

1905.01 P.g. ca. 198.052

Name: *Ġōr aṣ-Ṣāfi*.

Description: Tombs with EB IV/MB I pottery on surface on E edge of the *Wādi al-ʿAraba* ca. 5km S of Dead Sea.

¶ Frank, ZDPV 57, 1934, 204-06, Pl 21A; Glueck, AASOR 15, 1934-35, 7-9; Glueck, HUCA 11, 1936, 145.

2105.01 P.g. 2115.0540

Name: *Fuqēqis*.

Description: Large EB IV/MB I settlement with much pottery on top of hill ca. 1km NE of *Wādi Ḫuḍēra*.

¶ Glueck, EEP III, p. 94.

2105.02 P.g. 2130.0503

Name: *Al-Mudawwara*.

Description: Large EB IV/MB I settlement on plateau above and ca. 300m SW of *Wādi al-Muqēr*.

¶ Glueck, EEP III, p. 90.

9404.01 P.g. 9446.0488

Name: None.

Description: LB settlement (ca. 25 dunams) on sand dunes, ca. 7km from coast with Egyptian pottery from 19-23 dyn. and Palestinian LB III ware.

¶ Margovsky, Survey of North Sinai; Survey of Israel: IDA.

9404.02 P.g. 9441.0485

Name: None.

Description: Large area (ca. 10 dunams) on sand dunes, ca. 7km from coast with Egyptian pottery from 18-20 dyn. and Palestinian LB II-III ware.

¶ Margovsky, Survey of North Sinai; Survey of Israel: IDA.

9404.03 P.g. 9446.0481

Name: None.

Description: Small area (ca. 30 x 40m) on sand dunes ca. 7km from coast with pottery from LB II-III and 18-20th dyn.

¶ Margovsky, Survey of North Sinai; Survey of Israel: IDA.

9504.01 P.g. 9555.0488

Name: None.

Description: Mound (ca. 2 dunams) on sand dunes ca. 5km from coast with Egyptian pottery from 18-20th dyn.

¶ Margovsky, Survey of North Sinai; Survey of Israel: IDA.

9504.02 P.g. 9555.0486

Name: None.

Description: Scattered remains on sand dunes ca. 5km from coast with Egyptian pottery from 18th-20th dyn.

¶ Margovsky, Survey of North Sinai: IDA.

9504.03 P.g. 9557.0485

Name: None.

Description: Area on sand dunes ca. 5km from coast with many LB II-III and some Egyptian pottery.

¶ Survey of Israel: IDA.

9504.04 P.g. 9560.0485

Name: None.

Description: Large area on sand dunes ca. 5km from sea with LB pottery.

¶ Survey of Israel: IDA.

9504.05 P.g. 9560.0480

Name: None.

Description: Very large area (ca. 40 dunams) ca. 5 1/2km from coast with Egyptian pottery from the 18th-20th dyn. and Palestinian LB II-III ware.

¶ Margovsky, Survey of North Sinai; Survey of Israel: IDA.

9604.01 P.g. 9641.0493

Name: None.

Description: Very large area with much Chalcolithic-EB I pottery ca. 5km from coast.

¶ Margovsky, Survey of North Sinai: IDA.

9604.02 P.g. 9644.0493

Name: None.

Description: Very large mound (ca. 30 dunams) on sand dunes ca. 5km from coast with pottery from EB, EB IV/MB I, MB II and some Egyptian, possibly Middle Kingdom, pottery.

¶ Survey of Israel: IDA.

9604.03 P.g. 9644.0486

Name: None.

Description: Large mound ca. 15 dunams on sand dunes ca. 6km from coast, with EB, EB IV/MB I and possibly MB II pottery.

¶ Margovsky, Survey of North Sinai; Survey of Israel: IDA.

1204.01 P.g. 1295.0493

Name: None.

Description: EB IV/MB I remains in hills ca. 3/4km W of *Naḥal ᵓĀṭadim (Wādi al-ᶜAusaǧī).*

¶ Isr. Gen. Archives: IDA.

1204.02 P.g. 1263.0490

Name: None.

Description: EB IV/MB I remains in hills ca. 1km N of *Naḥal Rəvivim (Wādi ᶜUslūǧ).*

¶ Isr. Gen. Archives: IDA.

1304.01 P.g. 1314.0455

Name: *Ḫ. Umm Ǧrfn**.

Description: Large EB IV/MB I settlement on W bank of *Naḥal Mašᵓabim (Wādi Raḫama)* ca. 2km S of *Naḥal Rəvivim (Wādi Raḫama).*

¶ Survey of Negev: IDA.

1304.02 P.g. 1389.0456

Name: Gl 124.

Description: EB II pottery found in the *Naḥal Rəvivim (Wādi Raḫama).*

¶ Glueck, BASOR 138, 1955, 11; idem, BASOR 142, 1956, 17; Survey of Negev: IDA.

1304.03 P.g. 1398.0442

Name: Gl 123.

Description: Settlement on low hill at edge of valley ca. 300m from

---

*Transcription? Transcription here follows PEF 1:250.000 map.

(1304.03)

small lake with much EB IV/MB I pottery and a few sherds from EB I.

¶ Glueck, BASOR 138, 1955, 10; Survey of Negev: IDA.

1304.04 P.g. 1382-93.0427-41

Name: Gl 361 A-G, *Har Raḥama, Tel Yeroḥam (Tall Raḫama), Har Yeroḥam (Ǧ. Raḫama).*

Description: Very large EB IV/MB I settlement with round and rectangular houses, tumuli, burials. 2 levels excavated.

¶ RB 63, 1956, 86; Glueck, BASOR 149, 1958, 10; idem, BASOR 152, 1958, 19; RB 70, 1963, 563-65; Kochavi, BIES 13, 1963, 141f; Had. Arch., 1963, 9-11; Weippert, ZDPV 80, 1964, 160; Glueck, BASOR 179, 1965, 11; Rothenberg, ZN, 1967, 104; Kochavi, The Settlement of the Negev in the MB I Age (Hebrew Univ. Diss., 1967); Qadmoniot 2, 1969, 38ff; EAEHL I, 136f.

1404.01 P.g. 1485.0475

Name: None.

Description: Scattered remains with pottery and flints from EB IV/MB I on surface on plateau ca. 300m N of *Naḥal Refed (Wādi Raḫama).*

¶ Isr. Gen. Archives: IDA.

1404.02 P.g. 1485.0473

Name: *Giv'at Refed (az-Zūfā').*

Description: EB IV/MB I settlement on low mound on plateau, on N side of *Naḥal Refed (Wādi Raḫama).*

¶ Isr. Gen. Archives: IDA.

1404.03 P.g. 1474.0459

Name: None.

Description: EB IV/MB I settlement, with much pottery and flints, S of *Naḥal Refed (Wādi al Ǧurf).*

¶ Isr. Gen. Archives: IDA.

1404.04 P.g. 1410.0455

Name: Gl 120, *"Ḫ. Raḫama"*.

Description: Large settlement on slopes of long hill ca. 700m N of *Naḥal Yəroḥām (Wādi al Ǧurf)*. Much pottery from EB IV/MB I; some EB I sherds.

¶ Glueck, BASOR 138, 1955, 9f. 17; Isr. Gen. Archives: IDA.

1404.05 P.g. 1408.0450

Name: None.

Description: EB IV/MB I remains with stone circles on edge of valley on N side of *Naḥal Yəroḥām (Wādi al Ǧurf)*.

¶ Survey of Negev: IDA.

1404.06 P.g. 1475.0449

Name: Gl 310.

Description: EB IV/MB I settlement with much pottery ca. 1 1/4km NE of *Naḥal ʾAvnon (Wādi al Ǧurf)*.

¶ Glueck, BASOR 145, 1957, 14; idem, BASOR 152, 1959, 19.

1404.07 P.g. 1492.0443

Name: Gl 307.

Description: EB IV/MB I settlement with much pottery above and to the N of *Ha-Maḵteš Ha-Gādol (Wādi Ḥaṯīra)*.

¶ Glueck, BASOR 145, 1957, 14; idem, BASOR 152, 1959, 19; Survey of Negev: IDA.

1404.08 P.g. 1468.0442

Name: None.

Description: Very large EB IV/MB I settlement on 3 hills with about 50 stone circles on N side of *Naḥal ʾAvnon (Wādi al Ǧurf)*.

¶ Isr. Gen. Archives: IDA.

1404.09 P.g. 1449.0415

Name: None.

Description: EB IV/MB I settlement with 7 stone circles ca. 1/2km N

(1404.09)

of *Naḥal Šuʿȧlim (Wādi al Ğurf)* above and about 1 1/2km NW of *Ha-Maktẹš Ha-Gȧdol (Wādi Ḥaṯīra)*.

¶ Isr. Gen. Archives: IDA.

1404.10 P.g. 1443.0402

Name: None.

Description: EB IV/MB I settlement with 17 stone circles in a fork of *Naḥal Šuʿȧlim (Wādi al Ğurf)*, about 1km NW of *Ha-Maktẹš Ha-Gȧdol (Wādi Ḥaṯīra)*.

¶ Isr. Gen. Archives: IDA.

1504.01 P.g. 1585.0494

Name: None.

Description: EB IV/MB I settlement on top of hill ca. 1km S of *Naḥal ʾEfʿe (Wādi Faiʾ)*.

¶ Isr. Gen. Archives: IDA.

1504.02 P.g. 1575.0491

Name: None.

Description: EB IV/MB I tumuli at edge of hills ca. 1km SSE of *Naḥal ʾEfʿe (Wādi Faiʾ)*.

¶ Isr. Gen. Archives: IDA.

1504.03 P.g. 1580.0488

Name: None.

Description: EB IV/MB I settlement with stone circles in hills ca. 1 1/2km NE of *Naḥal Mamšit (Wādi Yerga*)*.

¶ Isr. Gen. Archives: IDA.

1504.04 P.g. 156.048

Name: *Ḥ. Mamšit (Kurnub)*.

Description: Small EB or Chalcolithic-EB I settlement on *Naḥal Mamšit*

---

* Transcription? Transcription here follows PEF 1: 250.000 map.

(Wādi Yerga).*

¶ Guy, QDAP 8, 1939, 169; Glueck, AJA 43, 1939, 151.

1504.05 P.g. 157.048

Name: None.

Description: Scattered remains with pottery from EB IV/MB I in hills ca. 1/2km NE of *Naḥal Mamšit (Wādi Yerga*).*

¶ Isr. Gen. Archives: IDA.

1504.06 P.g. 1567.0471

Name: None.

Description: Scattered remains with pottery from EB IV/MB I in hills ca. 1/2km N of *Naḥal Mamšit (Wādi Yerga*).*

¶ Isr. Gen. Archives: IDA.

1504.07 P.g. 1577.0476

Name: None.

Description: Scattered remains with EB IV/MB I pottery ca. 3/4km WNW of *Naḥal Mamšit (Wādi Yerga*)*; some possibly MB II pottery.

¶ Survey of Negev: IDA.

1504.08 P.g. 1506.0468

Name: None.

Description: Large EB IV/MB I settlement on NE bank of *Naḥal Refed (Wādi as-Sīr).*

¶ Isr. Gen. Archives: IDA.

1504.09 P.g. 1504.0461

Name: Gl 305.

Description: Small EB IV/MB I settlement on SW bank of *Naḥal Refed*

---

* Transcription? Transcription here follows PEF 1:250.000 map.

(1504.09)

(Wādi as-Sīr).

¶ Glueck, BASOR 145, 1957, 14; Survey of Negev: IDA.

1504.10 P.g. 1585.0434

Name: None.

Description: Scattered remains with EB IV/MB I pottery on small tributary of *Naḥal Yámin (Wādi Yaman).*

¶ Isr. Gen. Archives: IDA.

1704.01 P.g. 1798.0441

Name: Roth 53.

Description: Neolithic site (100 x 100m) with some LB/EI pottery.

¶ Rothenberg, Sfunot Negev, 119; further, courtesy of B. Rothenberg.

1704.02 P.g. 1797.0447

Name: Roth 54.

Description: Scattered remains with some LB/EI pottery.

¶ Rothenberg, Sfunot Negev, 119f; further, courtesy of B. Rothenberg.

1804.01 P.g. 1804.0467

Name: Roth 56.

Description: Small metallurgical site with some LB/EI pottery.

¶ Rothenberg, Sfunot Negev, 121f; further, courtesy of B. Rothenberg.

1804.02 P.g. 1805.0453

Name: None.

Description: Remains from EB IV/MB I at 3 different loci: 1805.0452, 1805.0453, and 1805.0455.

¶ Rothenberg, Sfunot Negev, 122f.

1804.03 P.g. 1832.0439

Name: Roth 50B.

Description: Scattered remains just W of *ʿEn Tåmår* with some possibly LB/EI pottery.

¶ Courtesy of B. Rothenberg.

1804.04 P.g. 1833.0437

Name: Roth 67, 67A, *ʿEn Tåmår*.

Description: Remains from EB II, EB IV/MB I and LB/EI ca. 150m SW of spring on the edge of *Ha-ʿĂråvå (Wādi al ʿAraba)*.

¶ Rothenberg, Das heilige Land 95, 1963, 23; idem, Sfunot Negev, 115; further, courtesy of B. Rothenberg.

1904.01 P.g. 194.049

Name: None.

Description: Tombs from EB IV/MB I found near *aṣ-Ṣāfi*.

¶ Glueck, EEP II, 8.

2004.01 P.g. 200.040

Name: *Ǧ. aḏ Dirāʿ*.

Description: Probable cemetery. Pottery from EB and MB II.

¶ British Mandate Archives: Pal. Mus.: IDA.

2104.01 P.g. 2140.0480

Name: Gl III 88, *Ḫ. aṣ-Ṣerâreh**.

Description: Small settlement with much EB IV/MB I pottery.

¶ Glueck, EEP III, 84.

2104.02 P.g. 2130.0470

Name: Gl III 87, *Ḫ. Umm aṣ-Sudēra*.

Description: Scattered remains immediately above and NW of *ʿAin Ǧāba*.

---

* Transcription? Here following Glueck.

(2104.02)

Very much pottery from EB and EB IV/MB I.

¶ Glueck, EEP III, 82.

2204.01 P.g. 2240.0430

Name: Gl 221, *Al-ʿAina*.

Description: Large EB IV/MB I settlement N of *al-ʿAina*, NE and NW of two springs. Much pottery found.

¶ Thomsen, ZDPV 29, 1906, 114; Glueck, BASOR, 65, 1937, 21f; idem, EEP II, 103.

1003.01 P.g. 1074.0379

Name: Gl 373.

Description: EB IV/MB I settlement on the *Naḥal Sidrȧ (Wādi Isdarīya)*.

¶ Glueck, BASOR 149, 1958, 17; Survey of Negev: IDA.

1003.02 P.g. 1059.0358

Name: Gl 372.

Description: EB IV/MB I settlement on W side of *Naḥal Sidrȧ (Wādi Isdarīya)*.

¶ Glueck, BASOR 149, 1958, 17; Survey of Negev: IDA.

1003.03 P.g. 1041.0317

Name: None.

Description: Scattered remains with EB IV/MB I pottery on N side of *Naḥal Rȧviv (Wādi Qaṯērī)*.

¶ Isr. Gen. Archives: IDA.

1103.01 P.g. 1110.0391

Name: None.

Description: EB IV/MB I remains near small unnamed wādi.

¶ Isr. Gen. Archives: IDA.

1103.02 P.g. 1138.0337

Name: None.

Description: EB IV/MB I settlement with stone circles on a small hill near tributary of *Naḥal Qorḥá (Wādi el Migrin*).*

¶ Survey of Negev: IDA.

1103.03 P.g. 1198.0337

Name: None.

Description: EB IV/MB I settlement on N side of *Naḥal Maśurá (Wādi az-Zayyātīn).*

¶ Isr. Gen. Archives: IDA.

1103.04 P.g. 1198.0334

Name: None.

Description: Scattered remains with pottery from EB IV/MB I on hill N and S of *Naḥal Maśurá (Wādi az-Zayyātīn).*

¶ Isr. Gen. Archives: IDA.

1203.01 P.g. 1243.0392

Name: None.

Description: Large EB IV/MB I settlement on hill ca. 3/4km N of *Naḥal Zalzal (Wādi Theigat el ʿAmirin*).*

¶ Survey of Israel: IDA.

1203.02 P.g. 12512.03970

Name: None.

Description: Scattered remains with EB IV/MB I pottery in hills NNE of *Naḥal Zalzal (Wādi Theigat el ʿAmirin*).*

¶ Survey of Israel: IDA.

1203.03 P.g. 12730.03950

Name: None.

Description: Stone circle on low hill with EB IV/MB I pottery along

* Transcription? Here following PEF 1:250.000 map.

(1203.03)

bank of small unnamed wādi.

¶ Survey of Israel: IDA.

1203.04 P.g. 12949.03930

Name: None.

Description: Scattered remains with EB IV/MB I pottery on hill ca. 2 1/2km N of *Naḥal Boqer (Wādi al-Baqqār)* on W side of *Naḥal Bəer Ḥayil (Wādi Umm Ḫarūba)*.

¶ Survey of Israel: IDA.

1203.05 P.g. 12942.03903

Name: None.

Description: Stone circle with EB IV/MB I pottery ca. 2 1/4km N of *Naḥal Boqer (Wādi al-Baqqār)*, on W side of *Naḥal Bəer Ḥayil (Wādi Umm Ḫarūba)*.

¶ Survey of Israel: IDA.

1203.06 P.g. 12125.03890

Name: None.

Description: Scattered remains with EB IV/MB I pottery on W side of *Naḥal Bəśor (Wādi Theigat el ʿAmirin*)*.

¶ Survey of Israel: IDA.

1203.07 P.g. 12320.03870

Name: None.

Description: Scattered remains with some EB IV/MB I pottery on hill ca. 900m N of *Naḥal Zalzal (Wādi Theigat el ʿAmirin*)*.

¶ Survey of Israel: IDA.

1203.08 P.g. 1239.0389

Name: None.

Description: EB IV/MB I settlement with 12 stone circles ca. 3/4km

---

*Transcription? Here following PEF 1:250.000 map.

(1203.08)

N of *Naḥal Zalzal (Wādi Theigat el ᶜAmirin*).*

¶ Survey of Israel: IDA.

1203.09 P.g. 12734.03832

Name: None.

Description: Scattered remains with EB IV/MB I pottery on the slopes of hill above *Naḥal Bəẹr Ḥayil (Wādi Imsura*)* and *Naḥal Bəśor (Wādi Theigat el ᶜAmirin*).*

¶ Survey of Israel: IDA.

1203.10 P.g. 12934.03887

Name: None.

Description: EB IV/MB I settlement on top of *Ramat Boqẹr (al-Baqqār).*

¶ Survey of Israel: IDA.

1203.11 P.g. 12093.03730

Name: None.

Description: Stone circles with EB IV/MB I pottery on hill along W side of *Naḥal Bəśor (Wādi Theigat el ᶜAmirin*).*

¶ Survey of Israel: IDA.

1203.12 P.g. 1200.0370

Name: None.

Description: EB IV/MB I remains with pottery and flints in hills ca. 1km W of *Naḥal Bəśor (Wādi Theigat el ᶜAmirin*).*

¶ Survey of Israel: IDA.

1203.13 P.g. 1224.0365

Name: None.

Description: Stone enclosure with EB IV/MB I pottery ca. 1/2km NE of *Naḥal Bəśor (Wādi Theigat el ᶜAmirin*).*

---

* Transcription? Here following PEF 1:250.000 map.

(1203.13)

¶ Survey of Israel: IDA.

1203.14 P.g. 12322.03684

Name: None.

Description: EB IV/MB I remains on low rise on bank of small tributary of *Naḥal Zalzal (Wādi Theigat el ʿAmirin*)*.

¶ Survey of Israel: IDA.

1203.15 P.g. 1234.0350

Name: None.

Description: EB IV/MB I remains on bank of *Naḥal Bəśor (Wādi Theigat el ʿAmirin*)*.

¶ Survey of Israel: IDA.

1203.16 P.g. 1296.0359

Name: None.

Description: EB IV/MB I settlement with many stones and pottery on N bank of tributary of *Naḥal Boqẹr (Wādi Umm Ḫarūba)*.

¶ Survey of Israel: IDA.

1203.17 P.g. 1297.0357

Name: None.

Description: EB IV/MB I remains on SW bank of tributary of *Naḥal Boqẹr (Wādi Umm Ḫarūba)*.

¶ Courtesy of R. Cohen: IDA.

1203.18 P.g. 12975.03550

Name: None.

Description: EB IV/MB I settlement with many flints (ca. 6000m²) on small tributary wādi of *Naḥal Boqẹr (Wādi Umm Ḫarūba)*.

¶ Southern Methodist University Expedition to the Negev, 1969; Isr. Gen. Archives: IDA.

---

*Transcription? Here following PEF 1:250.000 map.

1203.19 P.g. 1297.0354

Name: None.

Description: 2 stone circles with pottery from EB IV/MB I on tributary of *Naḥal Boqer (Wadi Umm Ḫarūba).*

¶ Survey of Israel: IDA.

1203.20 P.g. 1299.0353-4

Name: *Ḥ. Naḥal Boqer.*

Description: Very large EB IV/MB I settlement (ca. 20 dunams) on 3 hills with about 65 stone circles with many flints and pottery - on tributary of *Naḥal Boqer (Wādi Umm Ḫarūba).*

¶ Isr. Gen. Archives; Survey of Negev: IDA; Had. Arch. 4, 1965, 1.

1203.21 P.g. 1283.0332

Name: None.

Description: EB IV/MB I remains on *Naḥal Hårocå (Wādi Ḥalēqūm).*

¶ Isr. Gen. Archives: IDA.

1203.22 P.g. 1291.0337

Name: None.

Description: Scattered remains with possibly EB IV/MB I pottery on top of hill ca. 3/4km E of *Naḥal Hårocå (Wādi Halequm).*

¶ Survey of Israel: IDA.

1203.23 P.g. 1292.0322

Name: None.

Description: Scattered remains with EB IV/MB I pottery above and ca. 1/4km NE of *Naḥal Hårocå (Wādi Ḥalēqūm).*

¶ Isr. Gen. Archives; Survey of Negev: IDA.

1203.24 P.g. 1299.0328

Name: None.

Description: 3 stone circles with EB IV/MB I pottery in hills ca. 1km N of *Naḥal Hårocå (Wādi Ḥalēqūm).*

¶ Survey of Negev: IDA.

1203.25 P.g. 1227-8.0316

Name: None.

Description: Scattered remains with EB IV/MB I flints and pottery on *Har Boqẹr*.

¶ Survey of Israel: IDA.

1203.26 P.g. 12358.03108

Name: None.

Description: Scattered remains with EB IV/MB I pottery on *Har Boqẹr*.

¶ Survey of Israel: IDA.

1203.27 P.g. 1285.0318

Name: None.

Description: Scattered remains with EB IV/MB I pottery on slopes of hill ca. 3-400m SW of *Naḥal Ḥȧroᶜȧ (Wādi Ḥalēqūm)*.

¶ Survey of Israel: IDA.

1203.28 P.g. 1288.0317

Name: None.

Description: Stone circle with EB IV/MB I pottery on slopes of hill ca. 1/4km SW of *Naḥal Ḥȧroᶜȧ (Wādi Ḥalēqūm)*.

¶ Survey of Israel: IDA.

1203.29 P.g. 1287.0314

Name: None.

Description: Scattered remains with EB IV/MB I pottery along slopes of hill ca. 1/2km SW of *Naḥal Ḥȧroᶜȧ (Wādi Ḥalēqūm)*.

¶ Survey of Israel: IDA.

1203.30 P.g. 1284.0310

Name: None.

Description: Small EB IV/MB I settlement with 2 stone circles ca. 1 1/4km SW of *Naḥal Ḥȧroᶜȧ (Wādi Ḥalēqūm)*.

¶ Survey of Negev: IDA.

1203.31 P.g. 1286.0311

Name: None.

Description: Small EB IV/MB I settlement with 2 small stone circles on S slopes of hill ca. 1km SW of *Naḥal Ḥåroʿå (Wādi Ḥalēqūm)*.

¶ Survey of Israel: IDA.

1203.32 P.g. 1263.0307

Name: None.

Description: EB IV/MB I settlement on edge of hills ca. 3/4km E of *Naḥal Ṣippŏrim (Wādi al-Baqara)*.

¶ Isr. Gen. Archives: IDA.

1203.33 P.g. 1270.0300

Name: None.

Description: Scattered remains with EB IV/MB I pottery ca. 3 1/2km N of *ʿEn ʿÅvdat (ʿAin ʿAbda)*.

¶ Isr. Gen. Archives: IDA.

1203.34 P.g. 1275.0301

Name: None.

Description: Small EB IV/MB I settlement with 3 stone circles in hills ca. 2 1/2km N of *Naḥal Ṣin (Wādi al-Marra)* and 3 1/2km N of *ʿEn ʿÅvdat (ʿAin ʿAbda)*.

¶ Survey of Negev: IDA.

1203.35 P.g. 1283.0309

Name: None.

Description: Tumuli with EB IV/MB I pottery (cf. 1203.30).

¶ Survey of Israel: IDA.

1203.36 P.g. 1286.0309

Name: None.

Description: Stone circle and tumulus with EB IV/MB I pottery (cf. 1203.30.31).

¶ Survey of Israel: IDA.

1303.01 P.g. 1331.0391

Name: None.

Description: EB IV/MB I settlement on high hill just N of *Naḥal Boqẹr (Wādi al-Baqqār)*.

¶ Isr. Gen. Archives: IDA; Survey of Israel: IDA.

1303.02 P.g. 13422.03912

Name: None.

Description: Scattered remains with EB IV/MB I pottery along bank of *Naḥal Boqẹr (Wādi al-Baqqār)*.

¶ Survey of Israel: IDA.

1303.03 P.g. 1346.0393

Name: None.

Description: Scattered remains with EB IV/MB I pottery on hill on N bank of *Naḥal Boqẹr (Wādi al-Baqqār)*.

¶ Survey of Israel: IDA.

1303.04 P.g. 1358.0398

Name: None.

Description: Scattered remains with EB IV/MB I pottery along N bank of tributary of *Naḥal Rəvivim (Wādi al-Ǧurf)*, with tumuli and burials.

¶ Survey of Israel: IDA.

1303.05 P.g. 1366.0393

Name: None.

Description: Scattered remains with EB IV/MB I pottery along bank of tributary to *Naḥal Rəvivim (Wādi al-Ǧurf)*: more EB IV/MB I pottery found on hill nearby: P.g. 1367.0393.

¶ Survey of Israel: IDA.

1303.06 P.g. 1322.0388

Name: None.

Description: Scattered remains with EB IV/MB I pottery along bank of tributary to *Naḥal Boqẹr (Wādi al-Baqqār)*.

¶ Survey of Israel: IDA.

1303.07 P.g. 1333.0385

Name: None.

Description: Scattered remains with EB IV/MB I pottery on slopes of hill ca. 1km NW of *Naḥal Boqẹr (Wādi al-Baqqār).*

¶ Survey of Israel: IDA.

1303.08 P.g. 1350.0386

Name: None.

Description: Scattered remains with EB IV/MB I pottery near fork of *Naḥal Boqẹr (Wādi al-Baqqār).*

¶ Survey of Israel: IDA.

1303.09 P.g. 1353.0388

Name: None.

Description: Scattered remains with EB IV/MB I pottery and tumuli on branch of *Naḥal Boqẹr (Wādi al-Baqqār).*

¶ Survey of Israel: IDA.

1303.10 P.g. 1354.0386.

Name: None.

Description: Scattered remains with EB IV/MB I pottery on slopes of hill near tributary of *Naḥal ʾAḥdir (Wādi ʿArāǧīn).* More EB IV/MB I pottery on summit of hill: 1354.0385.

¶ Survey of Israel: IDA.

1303.11 P.g. 1357.0384

Name: None.

Description: Scattered remains with EB IV/MB I pottery on top of hill ca. 1km NW of *Naḥal ʾAḥdir (Wādi ʿArāǧīn).*

¶ Survey of Israel: IDA.

1303.12 P.g. 1357.0387

Name: None.

Description: Scattered remains with EB IV/MB I pottery on top of hill near tributary of *Naḥal ʾAḥdir (Wādi ʿArāǧīn).*

(1303.12)

¶ Survey of Israel: IDA.

1303.13 P.g. 1356.0382

Name: None.

Description: Scattered remains with EB IV/MB I pottery and tumuli on summit of hill above *Naḥal Boqer (Wādi al-Baqqār)*.

¶ Survey of Israel: IDA.

1303.14 P.g. 1359.0386

Name: None.

Description: Scattered remains with EB IV/MB I pottery and tumulus near tributary of *Naḥal ʾAḥdir (Wādi ʿArāǧīn)*.

¶ Survey of Israel: IDA.

1303.15 P.g. 1361.0384

Name: None.

Description: Scattered remains with EB IV/MB I pottery on hill near tributary of *Naḥal ʾAḥdir (Wādi ʿArāǧīn)*.

¶ Survey of Israel: IDA.

1303.16 P.g. 13755.03895

Name: None.

Description: Scattered remains with EB IV/MB I pottery on low mound along *Naḥal Rəvivim (Wādi al-Ǧurf)*.

¶ Survey of Israel: IDA.

1303.17 P.g. 1387.0379

Name: None.

Description: Small EB IV/MB I settlement on E bank of *Naḥal Rəvivim (Wādi al-Ǧurf)*.

¶ Survey of Israel: IDA.

1303.18 P.g. 1342.0365

Name: None.

Description: Small EB IV/MB I settlement on watershed between *Naḥal Boqer* and *Naḥal Ḥåroʿå (Wādi Ḥalēqūm)*.

¶ Survey of Israel: IDA.

1303.19 P.g. 1343.0360

Name: None.

Description: Scattered remains with EB IV/MB I pottery on top of hill below *Har Ḥalukim* ca. 1km NW of *Naḥal Ḥåroʿå (Wādi Ḥalēqūm)*.

¶ Survey of Israel: IDA.

1303.20 P.g. 1388.0365

Name: None.

Description: Scattered remains with EB IV/MB I pottery on top of hill above *Naḥal Rəvivim (Wādi al-Ǧurf)* and *Naḥal ʾAḥdir (Wādi ʿArāǧīn)*.

¶ Survey of Israel: IDA.

1303.21 P.g. 1386.0365

Name: None.

Description: Small EB IV/MB I settlement on slopes of hill above *Naḥal ʾAḥdir (Wādi ʿArāǧīn)*.

¶ Survey of Israel: IDA.

1303.22 P.g. 1386.0364.

Name: None.

Description: Small EB IV/MB I settlement on N bank of *Naḥal ʾAḥdir (Wādi ʿArāǧīn)*.

¶ Survey of Israel: IDA.

1303.23 P.g. 1385.0362

Name: None.

Description: Scattered remains with EB IV/MB I pottery on top of

(1303.23)

small hill along bank of *Naḥal ʾAḥdir (Wādi ʿArāǧīn).*

¶ Survey of Israel: IDA.

1303.24 P.g. 1383.0364

Name: None.

Description: Scattered remains with EB IV/MB I pottery on top of hill along the N bank of *Naḥal ʾAḥdir (Wādi ʿArāǧīn).*

¶ Survey of Israel: IDA.

1303.25 P.g. 1336.0354

Name: None.

Description: Scattered remains with EB IV/MB I pottery in hills ca. 1 1/4km NW of *Naḥal ʾAḥdir (Wādi ʿArāǧīn).*

¶ Survey of Israel: IDA.

1303.26 P.g. 1372.0357

Name: None.

Description: Scattered remains with EB IV/MB I pottery with tumulus and burial on top of hill along tributary to *Naḥal Ḥåroʿá (Wādi Ḥalēqūm).*

¶ Survey of Israel: IDA.

1303.27 P.g. 1387.0359

Name: None.

Description: Large EB IV/MB I settlement with many flints and pottery on N bank of *Naḥal ʾAḥdir (Wādi ʿArāǧīn).*

¶ Survey of Israel: IDA.

1303.28 P.g. 1391.0353

Name: None.

Description: Concentration of EB IV/MB I flints and pottery on low hill along the N bank of *Naḥal ʾAḥdir (Wādi ʿArāǧīn).*

¶ Survey of Israel: IDA.

1303.29 P.g. 1393.0352

Name: None.

Description: Small EB IV/MB I settlement with 5 round structures with many flints and pottery.

¶ Survey of Israel: IDA.

1303.30 P.g. 1370.0342

Name: None.

Description: Scattered remains with EB IV/MB I pottery on top of hill ca. 400-500m N of *Naḥal Ḥ̇aṩaṣ (Wādi ʿAraǧīn).*

¶ Survey of Israel: IDA.

1303.31 P.g. 1385.0344

Name: None.

Description: Scattered EB IV/MB I flints on top of hill ca. 1 1/4km N of *Naḥal Ḥ̇aṩaṣ (Wādi ʿAraǧīn).*

¶ Survey of Israel: IDA.

1303.32 P.g. 1392.0344

Name: None.

Description: Scattered remains with EB IV/MB I flints and pottery along the S bank of *Naḥal ʾAḥdir (Wādi ʿAraǧīn).*

¶ Survey of Israel: IDA.

1303.33 P.g. 1300.0334

Name: None.

Description: Scattered remains with EB IV/MB I pottery in hills ca. 1 1/2km N of *Naḥal Ḥ̊aroʿȧ (Wādi Ḥalēqūm).*

¶ Survey of Israel: IDA.

1303.34 P.g. 1303.0333

Name: None.

Description: Scattered remains with EB IV/MB I pottery on top of hill on E bank of tributary to *Naḥal Ḥ̊aroʿȧ (Wādi Ḥalēqūm).*

¶ Survey of Israel: IDA.

1303.35 P.g. 1354.0337

Name: None.

Description: Scattered remains with EB IV/MB I pottery and tumulus on hill to the N of *Naḥal Ḥáṣáṣ (Wādi ʿArāǧīn)*.

¶ Survey of Israel: IDA.

1303.36 P.g. 1354.0334

Name: None.

Description: Large EB IV/MB I settlement along the *Naḥal Ḥáṣáṣ (Wādi ʿArāǧīn)*.

¶ Survey of Israel: IDA.

1303.37 P.g. 1348.0323

Name: None.

Description: Scattered remains with EB IV/MB I pottery on top of hill along the N bank of tributary to *Naḥal Hároʿá (Wādi Ḥalēqūm)*.

¶ Survey of Israel: IDA.

1303.38 P.g. 1358.0323-4

Name: None.

Description: Scattered remains with EB IV/MB I pottery on top and slopes of hill along the N side of tributary to *Naḥal Hároʿá (Wādi Ḥalēqūm)*.

¶ Survey of Israel: IDA.

1303.39 P.g. 1343.0317

Name: None.

Description: Scattered remains with EB IV/MB I pottery on hill along the S bank of tributary to *Naḥal Hároʿá (Wādi Ḥalēqūm)*.

¶ Survey of Israel: IDA.

1303.40 P.g. 1371.0315

Name: None.

Description: 5 EB IV/MB I tombs.

(1303.40)

¶ Survey of Israel: IDA.

1303.41 P.g. 1312.0300

Name: None.

Description: Scattered remains with EB IV/MB I pottery on large plateau of *Śəde Ṣin (Naqb al-Ġārib)*.

¶ Survey of Israel: IDA.

1303.42 P.g. 1363.0308

Name: None.

Description: Scattered remains with EB IV/MB I pottery in hills ca. 350m S of tributary to *Naḥal Hårocå (Wādi Ḥalēqūm)*.

¶ Survey of Israel: IDA.

1303.43 P.g. 1369.0308

Name: None.

Description: Scattered remains with EB IV/MB I pottery on top of hill above *Naḥal Dårok̠ (Wādi al Maharug**) to the E.

¶ Survey of Israel: IDA.

1803.01 P.g. 1860.0377

Name: Roth 51.

Description: Metallurgical site on edge of *Ha-cĂrāvå (Wādi al-cAraba)* with some possibly LB/EI pottery.

¶ Rothenberg, Sfunot Negev, 117; further, courtesy of B. Rothenberg.

2103.01 P.g. 2131.0333

Name: *Ḫ. al-Mušimmīn,* Gl II 232.

Description: Settlement on the *Wādi Zafra*. Sherds from EB and EB IV/MB I.

¶ Glueck, EEP II, 104.

---

*Transcription? Here following PEF 1:250.000 map.

0902.01 P.g. 0982.0253

Name: None.

Description: Scattered remains with EB IV/MB I pottery along W bank of *Naḥal ᶜĔzuz (Wādi al-ᶜAuǧā᾽)*.

¶ Isr. Gen. Archives: IDA.

0902.02 P.g. 0983.0251

Name: None.

Description: Scattered remains with much EB IV/MB I pottery along W bank of *Naḥal ᶜĔzuz (Wādi al-ᶜAuǧā᾽)*.

¶ Isr. Gen. Archives: IDA.

0902.03 P.g. 0975.0247

Name: None.

Description: Small settlement (15 x 20m) with EB IV/MB I flints along E bank of *Naḥal Bǝẹrotayim (Wādi al-ᶜAuǧā᾽)*.

¶ Isr. Gen. Archives: IDA.

0902.04 P.g. 09890.02355

Name: Gl 330.

Description: EB IV/MB I settlement along W bank of *Naḥal ᶜĔzuz (Wādi al-ᶜAuǧā᾽)*.

¶ Glueck, BASOR 145, 1957, 19n33; Survey of Israel: IDA.

0902.05 P.g. 09975.02360

Name: Gl 330A.

Description: EB IV/MB I settlement along E bank of *Naḥal ᶜĔzuz (Wādi al-ᶜAuǧā᾽)*.

¶ Glueck, BASOR 145, 1957, 19; Survey of Negev: IDA.

0902.06 P.g. 0997.0233

Name: None.

Description: Small settlement (ca. 30 x 50m) along E bank of *Naḥal ᶜĔzuz (Wādi al-ᶜAuǧā᾽)*. Pottery from EB (few) and EB IV/MB I (many).

(0902.06)

¶ Isr. Gen. Archives: IDA.

0902.07 P.g. 0988.0227

Name: None.

Description: EB IV/MB I settlement with much pottery on E bank of *Naḥal Bəʾerotayim (Wādi al-ʿAuǧāʾ).*

¶ Isr. Gen. Archives: IDA.

0902.08 P.g. 0995.0221

Name: None.

Description: Small settlement (35 x 40m) with pottery and flints from EB (many) and possibly EB IV/MB I.

¶ Isr. Gen. Archives: IDA.

0902.09 P.g. 0998.0220

Name: Gl 329.

Description: EB IV/MB I settlement with much pottery on E bank of *Naḥal Bəʾerotayim (Wādi al-ʿAuǧāʾ).*

¶ Glueck, BASOR 145, 1957, 13. 19; Isr. Gen. Archives: IDA.

0902.10 P.g. 09880.02145

Name: Gl 164b.

Description: Very large EB IV/MB I settlement with large number of small buildings along W bank of *Naḥal Bəʾerotayim (Wādi al-ʿAuǧāʾ).*

¶ Glueck, BASOR 138, 1955, 20; Survey of Negev: IDA.

0902.11 P.g. 0996.0214

Name: Gl 164A.

Description: EB IV/MB I settlement with small buildings W of *Naḥal Bəʾerotayim (Wādi al-ʿAuǧāʾ).*

¶ Survey of Negev: IDA.

0902.12 P.g. 09925.02105

Name: Gl 337.

Description: EB IV/MB I settlement with much pottery on E bank of *Naḥal Bəẹrotayim (Wādi al-ʿAuǧā')*.

¶ Glueck, BASOR 145, 1957, 19n33; Survey of Negev: IDA.

0902.13 P.g. 0996.0201

Name: None.

Description: Small mound ca. 1/2km SW of *Naḥal Bəẹrotayim (Wādi al-ʿAuǧā')* with pottery and flints from EB IV/MB I (many) and possibly EB.

¶ Isr. Gen. Archives: IDA.

1002.01 P.g. 1073.0272

Name: None.

Description: Settlement on S bank of *Naḥal Rảviv (Wādi Qaṭērī)*. Pottery from EB IV/MB I (many) and possibly EB.

¶ Isr. Gen. Archives: IDA.

1002.02 P.g. 1010.0266

Name: Gl 367.

Description: EB IV/MB I cemetery in hills just to E of *Naḥal Niṣảnả (Wādi al-Ḥafīr)*.

¶ Glueck, BASOR 145, 1957, 19f; idem, BASOR 149, 1958, 11ff; idem, BASOR 152, 1958, 21-6; idem, BASOR 155, 1959, 4ff; Survey of Negev: IDA.

1002.03 P.g. 1020.0265 (Gl. field map ref.)

Name: Gl 369.

Description: Very large EB IV/MB I settlement in fork of *Naḥal Rut (Wādi Abu Rūḻa)*.

¶ Glueck, BASOR 149, 1958, 17; Survey of Negev: IDA.

1002.04 P.g. 1011.0245

Name: None.

Description: Scattered remains with EB IV/MB I pottery on W bank of

(1002.04)

Naḥal Niṣȧnȧ (Wādi al-Ḥafīr).

¶ Isr. Gen. Archives: IDA.

1002.05 P.g. 1015.0242

Name: None.

Description: Small EB IV/MB I settlement (30 x 42m) on *Naḥal Niṣȧnȧ (Wādi al-Ḥafīr).*

¶ Isr. Gen. Archives: IDA.

1002.06 P.g. 1015.0240

Name: None.

Description: Small EB IV/MB I settlement with much pottery along W bank of *Naḥal Niṣȧnȧ (Wādi al-Ḥafīr).*

¶ Isr. Gen. Archives: IDA.

1002.07 P.g. 1004.0231

Name: None.

Description: Scattered remains with EB IV/MB I pottery on tributary to *Naḥal ʿĔzuz (Wādi al-ʿAuǧāʾ)*, ca. 600m N of main wādi.

¶ Isr. Gen. Archives: IDA.

1002.08 P.g. 1008.0232

Name: Gl 330b.

Description: EB IV/MB I settlement on N bank of small tributary, ca. 1km N of *Naḥal ʿĔzuz (Wādi al-ʿAuǧāʾ).*

¶ Glueck, BASOR 145, 1957, 19n33; Survey of Negev: IDA.

1002.09 P.g. 10205.02310

Name: Gl 334.

Description: EB IV/MB I settlement with much pottery on W bank of *Naḥal Niṣȧnȧ (Wādi al-Ḥafīr).*

¶ Glueck, BASOR 145, 1957, 19; Survey of Negev: IDA.

1002.10 P.g. 10255.02220

Name: Gl 345.

Description: Very large EB IV/MB I settlement (ca. 1km x 200m) above W bank of *Naḥal Niṣánȧ (Wādi al-Ḥafīr)*.

¶ Glueck, BASOR 145, 1957, 19f; idem, BASOR 149, 1958, 15-17; idem, BASOR 159, 1960, 4; Survey of Negev: IDA.

1002.11 P.g. 1050.0216

Name: Gl 179.

Description: EB IV/MB I settlement with 3 large stone enclosures on N bank of *Naḥal Niṣánȧ (Wādi al-Ḥafīr)*.

¶ Glueck, BASOR 138, 1955, 19f; Survey of Negev: IDA.

1002.12 P.g. 10510.02125

Name: Gl 178.

Description: Very large EB IV/MB I settlement overlooking N bank of *Naḥal Niṣánȧ (Wādi al-Ḥafīr)*.

¶ Glueck, BASOR 138, 1955, 17ff; Isr. Gen. Archives: IDA.

1002.13 P.g. 1076.0214

Name: None.

Description: Large EB IV/MB I settlement with large stone enclosures ("desert kites") on three hills overlooking from the N the juncture of the *Naḥal Rəsisim (Wādi Rusēsīya)* and the *Naḥal Niṣánȧ (Wādi al-Ḥafīr)*.

¶ Isr. Gen. Archives: IDA.

1002.14 P.g. 1084.0212

Name: None.

Description: Large EB IV/MB I settlement with stone circles on bank of *Naḥal Rəsisim (Wādi Rusēsīya)*.

¶ Survey of Isr. Archives: IDA.

1002.15 P.g. 1005.0210

Name: Gl 331.

Description: Scattered remains with EB IV/MB I pottery on *Naḥal ʿĔzuz*

(1002.15)

(Wādi al-ʿAuǧāʾ).

¶ Glueck, BASOR 145, 1957, 19n33; Survey of Negev: IDA.

1002.16 P.g. 1090.0206

Name: *Bəẹr Rəsisim.*

Description: Very large EB IV/MB I settlement with ca. 130 separate structures along S side of *Naḥal Rəsisim (Wādi Rusēsīya)*, Many tumuli in surrounding hills.

¶ Kochavi, unpublished Hebrew University diss., 1965.

1002.17 P.g. 1094.0203

Name: None.

Description: Scattered remains over area (ca. 6 dunams) with EB IV/MB I pottery near *Naḥal Rəsisim (Wādi Rusēsīya).*

¶ Isr. Gen. Archives: IDA.

1102.01 P.g. 11860.02205

Name: None.

Description: Small EB IV/MB I settlement with stone circles on upper slopes of *Har Lȧvȧn (Rās al-Abyaḍ).*

¶ Survey of Israel: IDA.

1102.02 P.g. 1185.0221

Name: RM 150.

Description: Small EB IV/MB I settlement with buildings on upper slopes of *Har Lȧvȧn (Rās al-Abyaḍ).*

¶ Aharoni, IEJ 10, 1960, 25.

1102.03 P.g. 1188.0222

Name: RM 112.

Description: Small EB IV/MB I settlement with stone circles on upper slopes of *Har Lȧvȧn (Rās al-Abyaḍ).*

¶ Aharoni, IEJ 10, 1960, 25; Survey of Israel: IDA.

1102.04 P.g. 11910.02225

Name: RM 110.

Description: Large settlement of EB IV/MB I with buildings and tumuli on *Har Lávân (Rās al-Abyaḍ)*.

¶ Aharoni, IEJ 10, 1960, 25f; Survey of Israel: IDA.

1102.05 P.g. 11925.02230

Name: RM 111.

Description: Scattered remains with EB IV/MB I pottery and tumuli on *Har Lávân (Rās al-Abyaḍ)*.

¶ Aharoni, IEJ 10, 1960, 25; Survey of Israel: IDA.

1102.06 P.g. 11820.02195

Name: None.

Description: Scattered remains with EB IV/MB I pottery, stone circles, and 2 enclosures on upper slopes of *Har Lávân (Rās al-Abyaḍ)*.

¶ Survey of Israel: IDA.

1102.07 P.g. 11830.02195

Name: RM 177.

Description: Small EB IV/MB I settlement with stone circles and buildings on *Har Lávân (Rās al-Abyaḍ)*.

¶ Aharoni, IEJ 10, 1960, 25; Survey of Israel: IDA.

1102.08 P.g. 1182.0218

Name: RM 178.

Description: Small EB IV/MB I settlement with buildings on *Har Lávân (Rās al-Abyaḍ)*.

¶ Aharoni, IEJ 10, 1960, 25.

1102.09 P.g. 1184.0218

Name: RM 176.

Description: Small EB IV/MB I settlement with buildings on *Har Lávân (Rās al-Abyaḍ)*.

¶ Aharoni, IEJ 10, 1960, 25.

1102.10 P.g. 11850.02185

Name: None.

Description: Scattered remains with EB IV/MB I pottery and tumuli on *Har Lȧvȧn (Rās al-Abyaḍ).*

¶ Survey of Negev: IDA.

1102.11 P.g. 11955.02199

Name: None.

Description: Scattered remains with EB IV/MB I pottery and round circles on *Har Lȧvȧn (Rās al-Abyaḍ).*

¶ Survey of Israel: IDA.

1102.12 P.g. 11560.02045

Name: RM 182.

Description: Small EB IV/MB I settlement with stone circles and tumuli on upper slopes of *Har Lȧvȧn (Rās al-Abyaḍ).*

¶ Aharoni, IEJ 10, 1960, 25; Survey of Israel: IDA.

1102.13 P.g. 1167.0206

Name: RM 181.

Description: Small EB IV/MB I settlement with buildings on upper slopes of *Har Lȧvȧn (Rās al-Abyaḍ).*

¶ Aharoni, IEJ 10, 1960, 25.

1102.14 P.g. 11680.02075

Name: None.

Description: EB IV/MB I settlement with 2 large enclosures and ca. 10 stone circles on upper slopes of *Har Lȧvȧn (Rās al-Abyaḍ).*

¶ Survey of Israel: IDA.

1202.01 P.g. 1243-4.0291-3

Name: None.

Description: Large EB IV/MB I settlement with tumuli and much pottery on two hills along the *Nahal Beśor (Wādi Theigat el*

(1202.01)

ʿAmirin).*

¶ Survey of Israel: IDA.

1202.02 P.g. 1267.0298

Name: None.

Description: Scattered remains with EB IV/MB I pottery and 5 stone circles in hills ca. 1/2km SE of *Naḥal Bəśor (Wādi Theigat el ʿAmirin*).*

¶ Survey of Israel: IDA.

1202.03 P.g. 1269.0293

Name: None.

Description: Scattered remains with EB IV/MB I pottery and 4 stone circles above *Naḥal Ṣin (Wādi al-Marra).*

¶ Survey of Israel: IDA.

1202.04 P.g. 1254.0290 (Gl. field map ref.)

Name: Gl 79.

Description: Settlement with rectangular platform on top of hill and stone circles on E slope ca. 1/2km N of *Naḥal Bəśor (Wādi Theigat el ʿAmirin*).* Pottery from Chalcolithic-EB I, EB, EB IV/MB I.

¶ Glueck, BASOR 137, 1955, 16.

1202.05 P.g. 1258.0289 (Gl. field map ref.)

Name: Gl 66.

Description: Large EB IV/MB I settlement near top of hill, ca. 1/2km NE of *Naḥal Bəśor (Wādi Theigat el ʿAmirin*)*; also much pottery from Chalcolithic-EB I, and EB. Many EB IV/MB I burial cairns in surrounding hills.

¶ Glueck, BASOR 137, 1955, 11ff; idem, BASOR 138, 1955, 8, 17; Isr. Gen. Archives: IDA.

---

* Transcription? Here following PEF 1:250.000 map.

1202.06 P.g. 1264.0290

Name: Gl 80.

Description: Stone circles and small buildings on top and slopes of hill ca. 1 1/2km NE of *Naḥal Bəśor (Wādi Theigat el ʿAmirin*)*. Pottery from Chalcolithic-EB I, EB and EB IV/MB I (many).

¶ Glueck, BASOR 137, 1955, 16.

1202.07 P.g. 1204.0275

Name: Gl 188a.

Description: EB IV/MB I settlement with much pottery on the *Naḥal Ṣippŏrim (Wādi al-Abyaḍ)*.

¶ Glueck, BASOR 138, 1955, 17; Isr. Gen. Archives: IDA.

1202.08 P.g. 1225.0275**

Name: Gl 186a.

---

*Transcription? Here following PEF 1:250.000 map.

**It is difficult to ascertain the correct coordinates for this and the following sites: 1202.09.10.11.12 (Gl 186.186A.186B. 186C and 186D). Glueck's published description of the location of the sites (BASOR 138, 1955, 14-16) fits neither his published coordinates nor the notations on his field map (Cf. Thompson, ZDPV 91, 1975, in press). An added difficulty is that 186D is not marked on the field map. It is possible that Glueck's written description had been taken from field notes which were made independent of the marking of his field map, and that the published coordinates were derived from an inexact reading of the field map, and then partially corrected on the basis of the field notes. In any case, the field map coordinates for 186 and 186A seem better suited to the description of these sites as related to the SW end of *Naḥal Bəśor*, a b o v e and not i n *Naḥal Ṣippŏrim*. The location of 186B poses a major difficulty since the description best fits Glueck's published coordinates; only, however, when one assumes the location of 186 as given on the field map! The location of 186C and 186D in the description are dependent on the location of 186B. If the site descriptions are correct, the published coordinates for 186B, 186C, and 186D could be accepted. If the field maps, however, are to be considered, and generally they are to be preferred to Glueck's published coordinates, a solution to the difficulty presents itself when we understand the field map notations for 186B and 186C as referring in fact to 186C and 186D respectively, and suggest that through an oversight the notation for 186B (rather than 186D) had been left off the map. This would then fit both the field map and Glueck's published site description! 186B must lie approximately .25km SSE-SE of 186 and .5km NW-NNW of 186C (BASOR, 138, 16), i.e., approximately P.g. 1229.0267. The consistent error in Glueck's published coordinates is then to be understood as deriving from an inexact reading of the coordinates for 186 and 186A.

(1202.08)

Description: Stone circles with much EB IV/MB I pottery ca. 400m above the E bank of *Naḥal Ṣippŏrim (Wādi al-Abyaḍ)*, near the SW end of *Naḥal Bəśor (Wādi Theigat el ᶜAmirin*)*.

¶ Glueck, BASOR 138, 1955, 15f; Isr. Gen. Archives: IDA.

1202.09 P.g. 1228.0270

Name: Gl 186.

Description: EB IV/MB I settlement with much pottery; stone foundations over area ca. 35 x 75m. Site lies to the E and above the *Naḥal Ṣippŏrim (Wādi al-Abyaḍ)*.

¶ Glueck, BASOR 138, 1955, 14f; idem, BASOR 142, 1956, 21; Isr. Gen. Archives: IDA.

1202.10 P.g. 1229.0267

Name: Gl 186b.

Description: Scattered remains with EB IV/MB I pottery along E bank of *Naḥal Ṣippŏrim (Wādi al-Abyaḍ)*.

¶ Glueck, BASOR 138, 1955, 16; Isr. Gen. Archives: IDA.

1202.11 P.g. 1231.0262

Name: Gl 186c.

Description: Large EB IV/MB I settlement with stone circles and enclosures on small tributary to *Naḥal Ṣippŏrim (Wādi al-Abyaḍ)*.

¶ Glueck, BASOR 138, 1955, 16; Isr. Gen. Archives: IDA.

1202.12 P.g. 1232.0261

Name: Gl 186d.

Description: Scattered remains with much EB IV/MB I pottery and stone circles on tributary to *Naḥal Ṣippŏrim (Wādi al-Abyaḍ)*.

¶ Glueck, BASOR 138, 1955, 16; Isr. Gen. Archives: IDA.

---

*Transcription? Here following PEF 1:250.000 map.

1202.13 P.g. 12390.02665

Name: Gl 185.

Description: Small EB IV/MB I settlement with stone circles and much pottery on slopes of hill overlooking *Naḥal Bəśor (Wādi Theigat el ʿAmirin*)* from the E.

¶ Glueck, BASOR 138, 1955, 13f; Isr. Gen. Archives: IDA.

1202.14 P.g. 1243.0268**

Name: Gl 184a.

Description: Large EB IV/MB I settlement on gently rising slope along *Naḥal Bəśor (Wadi Theigat el Amirin*)*.

¶ Glueck, BASOR 138, 1955, 12f; idem, BASOR 142, 1956, 21; Isr. Gen. Archives: IDA.

1202.15 P.g. ca. 1242.0266***

Name: Gl 184b.

Description: Scattered remains with much EB IV/MB I pottery and many stone circles on ridge above *Naḥal Bəśor (Wādi Theigat el ʿAmirin*)*.

¶ Glueck, BASOR 138, 1955, 13; idem, BASOR 142, 1956, 21; Isr. Gen. Archives: IDA.

1202.16 P.g. 1264.0267

Name: None.

Description: EB IV/MB I settlement with 6 enclosures ca. 1km W of *ʿEn ʿAvdat (ʿAin ʿAbda)*.

¶ Isr. Gen. Archives: IDA.

1202.17 P.g. 1266.0266

Name: None.

---

* Transcription? Here following PEF 1:250.000 map.

** Field map reference for Gl 184!

*** This site does not appear on Glueck's field map. His published coordinate, however, does not fit his site description which suggests rather the coordinate given here.

(1202.17)

Description: Scattered remains with EB IV/MB I pottery and 2 stone circles ca. 3/4km W of *ʿEn ʿAvdat (ʿAin ʿAbda)*.

¶ Survey of Israel: IDA.

1202.18 P.g. 1238.0259

Name: None.

Description: Small EB IV/MB I settlement with single enclosure in hills above *Naḥal Bəśor (Wādi Theigat el ʿAmirin*)*.

¶ Isr. Gen. Archives; Survey of Israel: IDA.

1202.19 P.g. 1235.0252

Name: None.

Description: Scattered remains with EB IV/MB I pottery and stone enclosures in hills ca. 1 1/2 - 2km from *Naḥal Ṣippŏrim (Wādi al-Abyaḍ)*. Findspots: 12335.02520, 1235.0252, 1235.0254, 1236.0254.

¶ Isr. Gen. Archives; Survey of Negev: IDA.

1202.20 P.g. 1244.0258

Name: None.

Description: EB IV/MB I settlement with 6 stone circles and 5 enclosures on *Har Miḥyȧ (Ǧ. Mahawīya)* ca. 300m E of *Naḥal Bəśor (Wādi Theigat el ʿAmirin*)*.

¶ Survey of Negev; Isr. Gen. Archives: IDA.

1202.21 P.g. 1249.0258

Name: None.

Description: Scattered remains with pottery from EB (much) and EB IV/MB I on *Har Miḥyȧ (Ǧ. Mahawīya)*.

¶ Isr. Gen. Archives: IDA.

---

* Transcription? Here following PEF 1:250.000 map.

1202.22 P.g. 1243.0255

Name: None.

Description: Small EB IV/MB I settlement with 2 enclosures on *Har Miḥyȧ (Ǧ. Mahawīya)* ca. 1 3/4km E of *Naḥal Ṣippŏrim (Wādi al-Abyaḍ).*

¶ Survey of Israel; Isr. Gen. Archives: IDA.

1202.23 P.g. 1252.0259

Name: None.

Description: EB IV/MB I settlement on upper slopes of *Har Miḥyȧ (Ǧ. Mahawīya)* along small tributary to *Naḥal ʿȦvdat (Wādi ʿAbda).*

¶ Isr. Gen. Archives: IDA.

1202.24 P.g. 1253.0252

Name: None.

Description: Settlement on slopes of *Har Miḥyȧ (Ǧ. Mahawīya)* N of tributary to *Naḥal ʿȦvdat (Wādi ʿAbda).* Pottery from EB and EB IV/MB I.

¶ Isr. Gen. Archives: IDA.

1202.25 P.g. 12570.02505

Name: None.

Description: Small EB IV/MB I settlement with 2 enclosures along N side of tributary to *Naḥal ʿȦvdat (Wādi ʿAbda).* Find-spots: 1257.0252, 12560.02505.

¶ Survey of Israel; Isr. Gen. Archives: IDA.

1202.26 P.g. 1268.0258

Name: None.

Description: EB IV/MB I settlement with 6 stone circles and 2 enclosures along tributary to *Naḥal ʿȦvdat (Wādi ʿAbda)*; ca. 1/2km W of *ʿEn Maʿărif (ʿAin Murēfiq)* and ca. 1km SW of *ʿEn ʿȦvdat (ʿAin ʿAbda).*

¶ Survey of Israel; Isr. Gen. Archives: IDA.

1202.27 P.g. 12300.02475

Name: None.

Description: EB IV/MB I settlement with 15 stone circles on *Har Rətåmim (Naqb Umm Ratāma)*.

¶ Survey of Israel: IDA.

1202.28 P.g. 1234.0244

Name: None.

Description: EB IV/MB I settlement with 5 stone circles on *Har Rətåmim (Naqb Umm Ratāma)*.

¶ Isr. Gen. Archives; Survey of Israel: IDA.

1202.29 P.g. 12380.02425

Name: None.

Description: Large EB IV/MB I settlement with 24 stone circles on *Har Rətåmim (Naqb Umm Ratāma)*.

¶ Survey of Israel: IDA.

1202.30 P.g. 1238.0243

Name: None.

Description: EB IV/MB I settlement with 5 stone circles, 3 enclosure walls and 1 tumulus on *Har Rətåmim (Naqb Umm Ratāma)*.

¶ Isr. Gen. Archives: IDA.

1202.31 P.g. 1239.0243

Name: None.

Description: Scattered remains with EB IV/MB I pottery on *Har Rətåmim (Naqb Umm Ratāma)*.

¶ Isr. Gen. Archives: IDA.

1202.32 P.g. 1239.0245

Name: None.

Description: EB IV/MB I settlement with 6 stone circles and 3 enclosures on *Har Rətåmim (Naqb Umm Ratāma)*.

¶ Isr. Gen. Archives: IDA.

1202.33 P.g. 1240.0245

Name: None.

Description: Scattered remains with EB IV/MB I pottery on *Har Rətâmim (Naqb Umm Ratāma).*

¶ Isr. Gen. Archives: IDA.

1202.34 P.g. 123-4.024

Name: None.

Description: Scattered remains with EB pottery on slopes of *Har Rətâmim (Naqb Umm Ratāma)* above *Naḥal Rətâmim (Wādi ʿAbda).*

¶ Isr. Gen. Archives: IDA.

1202.35 P.g. 1242.0242

Name: None.

Description: EB IV/MB I settlement with 2 stone circles and 5 enclosures on *Har Rətâmim (Naqb Umm Ratāma).*

¶ Isr. Gen. Archives: IDA.

1202.36 P.g. 1251.0246

Name: Gl 301.

Description: EB IV/MB I settlement in hills on upper slopes of tributary to *Naḥal Rətâmim (Wādi ʿAbda).*

¶ Glueck, BASOR 145, 1957, 17; Isr. Gen. Archives: IDA.

1202.37 P.g. 1265.0247

Name: Gl 297.

Description: EB IV/MB I settlement just N of small tributary to *Naḥal ʿȦvdat (Wādi ʿAbda).*

¶ Glueck, BASOR 145, 1957, 17; Isr. Gen. Archives: IDA.

1202.38 P.g. 12385.02365

Name: None.

Description: EB IV/MB I settlement with 6 stone circles in hills near upper reaches of *Naḥal Rətâmim (Wādi ʿAbda).*

(1202.38)

¶ Survey of Israel: IDA.

1202.39 P.g. 12455.02380

Name: None.

Description: EB IV/MB I settlement on hill above and to N of *Naḥal Rətámim (Wādi ʿAbda)*. Stone circles and 9 enclosures found. Findspots: also 1246.0238, 1245.0238.

¶ Survey of Israel; Isr. Gen. Archives: IDA.

1202.40 P.g. 1247.0235

Name: None.

Description: Scattered remains with EB IV/MB I pottery near *Naḥal Rətámim (Wādi ʿAbda)* with 3 stone circles.

¶ Survey of Israel: IDA.

1202.41 P.g. 12475.02330

Name: None.

Description: EB IV/MB I settlement with 6 stone circles on bank of *Naḥal Rətámim (Wādi ʿAbda)*.

¶ Isr. Gen. Archives: IDA.

1202.42 P.g. 1249.0234

Name: None.

Description: EB IV/MB I settlement with 3 stone circles on hill above *Naḥal Rətámim (Wādi ʿAbda)*.

¶ Survey of Israel; Isr. Gen. Archives: IDA.

1202.43 P.g. 1250.0233

Name: Gl 302.

Description: EB IV/MB I settlement in hills on N bank of *Naḥal Rətámim (Wādi ʿAbda)*.

¶ Glueck, BASOR 145, 1957, 17.

1202.44 P.g. 1257.0235

Name: Gl 303.

Description: Large EB IV/MB I settlement in hills on N bank of *Naḥal Rətâmim (Wādi ʿAbda).*

¶ Glueck, BASOR 145, 1957, 17; Isr. Gen. Archives: IDA.

1202.45 P.g. 12550.02305

Name: None.

Description: Large EB IV/MB I settlement with 24 stone circles and 1 enclosure on *Naḥal Rətâmim (Wādi ʿAbda).*

¶ Isr. Gen. Archives: IDA.

1202.46 P.g. 1255.0235

Name: None.

Description: Scattered remains with EB IV/MB I pottery on hill N and above *Naḥal Rətâmim (Wādi ʿAbda).*

¶ Isr. Gen. Archives: IDA.

1202.47 P.g. 1259.0238

Name: None.

Description: Large EB IV/MB I settlement with 25 stone circles ca. 1/2km N of *Naḥal Rətâmim (Wādi ʿAbda).*

¶ Survey of Israel: IDA.

1202.48 P.g. 1261.0234

Name: None.

Description: EB IV/MB I settlement with 2 stone circles near *Naḥal Rətâmim (Wādi ʿAbda).*

¶ Survey of Israel: IDA.

1202.49 P.g. 1205.0229

Name: None.

Description: EB IV/MB I settlement with stone circles and buildings in hills.

¶ Aharoni, IEJ 10, 1960, 25; Survey of Israel: IDA.

1202.50 P.g. 1208.0222

Name: RM 132.

Description: EB IV/MB I settlement with stone circles and buildings in hills just S of *Naḥal Ṣippŏrim (Wādi al-Abyaḍ).*

¶ Aharoni, IEJ 10, 1960, 25; Survey of Israel: IDA.

1202.51 P.g. 12350.02265

Name: None.

Description: EB IV/MB I settlement with 6 stone circles on *Har ᶜArqov (Ǧ. Ergab Esdud*)*.

¶ Isr. Gen. Archives: IDA.

1202.52 P.g. 123-4.022

Name: None.

Description: EB settlement on slopes of *Har ᶜArqov (Ǧ. Ergab Esdud*)* ca. 1 3/4km N of *Naḥal ᶜȦvdat (Wādi ᶜAbda)*.

¶ Isr. Gen. Archives: IDA.

1202.53 P.g. 1244.0225

Name: None.

Description: EB IV/MB I settlement with 7 stone circles on *Har ᶜArqov (Ǧ. Ergab Esdud*)*.

¶ Survey of Israel: IDA.

1202.54 P.g. 1262.0222

Name: None.

Description: EB IV/MB I settlement with 5 stone circles on slope W of *Naḥal ᶜȦvdat (Wādi ᶜAbda)*.

¶ Survey of Israel: IDA.

1202.55 P.g. 1213.0210

Name: RM 161.

Description: EB IV/MB I settlement with stone circles and buildings

---

* Transcription? Here following PEF 1:250.000 map.

(1202.55)

along side of small tributary wādi.

¶ Aharoni, IEJ 10, 1960, 25.

1202.56 P.g. 1215.0214

Name: RM 154.

Description: EB IV/MB I settlement with stone circles and buildings along side of small tributary wādi.

¶ Aharoni, IEJ 10, 1960, 25.

1202.57 P.g. 12170.02145

Name: None.

Description: EB IV/MB I settlement with stone circles along side of small tributary wādis.

¶ Survey of Israel: IDA.

1202.58 P.g. 12185.02145

Name: RM 155.

Description: EB IV/MB I settlement with stone circles, buildings and tumuli near small tributary wādi.

¶ Aharoni, IEJ 10, 1960, 25; Survey of Israel: IDA.

1202.59 P.g. 12195.02140

Name: None.

Description: Scattered remains with EB IV/MB I pottery near small tributary wādi.

¶ Survey of Israel: IDA.

1202.60 P.g. 1220.0212

Name: RM 157.

Description: EB IV/MB I settlement with stones and building along side of small tributary wādi.

¶ Aharoni, IEJ 10, 1960, 25.

1202.61 P.g. 12215.02125

Name: None.

Description: Scattered remains with EB IV/MB I pottery with stone circles near small tributary wādi.

¶ Survey of Israel: IDA.

1202.62 P.g. 12355.02170

Name: None.

Description: Small EB IV/MB I settlement with 5 stone circles on slopes of *Har ʿȦrqov (Ǧ. Ergab Esdud*)* near tributary of *Naḥal ʿȦvdat (Wādi ʿAbda)*.

¶ Isr. Gen. Archives: IDA.

1202.63 P.g. 1236.0216

Name: None.

Description: EB remains on slopes of *Har ʿArqov (Ǧ. Ergab Esdud*)* near tributary of *Naḥal ʿȦvdat (Wādi ʿAbda)*.

¶ Isr. Gen. Archives: IDA.

1202.64 P.g. 12480.02175

Name: None.

Description: EB IV/MB I site with 7 stone circles and 3 enclosures on slopes of *Har ʿArqov (Ǧ. Ergab Esdud*)* near small tributary of *Naḥal ʿȦvdat (Wādi ʿAbda)*.

¶ Isr. Gen. Archives: IDA.

1202.65 P.g. 1249.0219

Name: None.

Description: EB IV/MB I site with 15 stone circles on slopes of *Har ʿArqov (Ǧ. Ergab Esdud*)* ca. 1km NW of *Naḥal ʿȦvdat (Wādi ʿAbda)*.

¶ Survey of Israel: IDA.

---

* Transcription? Here following PEF 1:250.000 map.

1202.66 P.g. 12450.02115

Name: None.

Description: EB IV/MB I site with remains of 7 courtyards and 1 large stone circle on slopes of *Har ʿArqov (Ǧ. Ergab Esdud*)* along tributary of *Naḥal ʿÅvdat (Wādi ʿAbda)*.

¶ Isr. Gen. Archives: IDA.

1202.67 P.g. 12550.02155

Name: None.

Description: EB IV/MB I settlement with 4 stone circles and 2 enclosures on hill on N side of *Naḥal ʿÅvdat (Wādi ʿAbda)*.

¶ Isr. Gen. Archives: IDA.

1202.68 P.g. 1257.0218

Name: None.

Description: Large EB IV/MB I settlement with many stone circles and 7 enclosures on N side of *Naḥal ʿÅvdat (Wādi ʿAbda)*.

¶ Survey of Negev: IDA.

1202.69 P.g. 12060.02085

Name: RM 139.

Description: Small EB IV/MB I settlement with enclosures and tumuli near upper tributaries to *Naḥal Maṭrẹd (Wādi al-Maṭrada)*.

¶ Aharoni, IEJ 10, 1960, 25.

1202.70 P.g. 12070.02075

Name: RM 152.

Description: EB IV/MB I settlement with stone circles and much pottery along tributary to *Naḥal Maṭrẹd (Wādi al-Maṭrada)*.

¶ Aharoni, IEJ 10, 1960, 25; Survey of Israel: IDA.

---

*Transcription? Here following PEF 1:250.000 map.

1202.71 P.g. 12150.02095

Name: None.

Description: EB IV/MB I settlement with 2 stone circles and scattered stones on slopes above *Naḥal Maṭreḏ (Wādi al-Maṭrada).*

¶ Survey of Israel: IDA.

1202.72 P.g. 12150.02065

Name: RM 162.

Description: Scattered remains with EB IV/MB I pottery and enclosure wall near upper tributaries to *Naḥal Maṭreḏ (Wādi al-Maṭrada).*

¶ Aharoni, IEJ 10, 1960, 25; Survey of Israel: IDA.

1202.73 P.g. 1216.0204

Name: RM 163.

Description: Scattered remains with EB IV/MB I pottery and tumuli on slopes above *Naḥal Maṭreḏ (Wādi al-Maṭrada).*

¶ Aharoni, IEJ 10, 1960, 25.

1202.74 P.g. 12185.02045

Name: None.

Description: Scattered remains with EB IV/MB I pottery, stone circle, and tumulus on slopes above *Naḥal Maṭreḏ (Wādi al-Maṭrada).*

¶ Survey of Israel: IDA.

1202.75 P.g. 12735.02070

Name: None.

Description: Scattered remains with EB IV/MB I pottery on *Har ʾEldȧd (Ǧ. an-Nafḫ)* ca. 1 1/2km S of fork on *Naḥal Ṣin (Wādi ʿAbda)* and *Naḥal ʿȦvdat (Wādi Raintīya).*

¶ Survey of Israel: IDA.

1202.76 P.g. 1275.0206

Name: None.

Description: Small EB IV/MB I settlement with 3 stone circles on

(1202.76)

Har ᵓEldād (Ǧ. an-Nafḫ) overlooking *Naḥal Ṣin (Wādi ᶜAbdā)* to the NE.

¶ Survey of Israel: IDA.

1202.77 P.g. 1276.0203

Name: None.

Description: Small EB IV/MB I settlement with 2 stone circles on *Har ᵓEldād (Ǧ. an-Nafḫ)* overlooking *Naḥal Ṣin (Wādi ᶜAbdā)* to the E.

¶ Survey of Israel: IDA.

1302.01 P.g. 1316.0294

Name: None.

Description: Scattered remains with EB IV/MB I pottery and flints in *Śədẹ Ṣin* to the E of tributary of *Naḥal Ṣin (Wādi al-Marra)*.

¶ Survey of Israel: IDA.

1302.02 P.g. 1312.0292

Name: None.

Description: Scattered remains with EB IV/MB I pottery in *Śədẹ Ṣin* on W side of tributary of *Naḥal Ṣin (Wādi al-Marra)*.

¶ Isr. Gen. Archives: IDA.

1302.03 P.g. 1365.0275

Name: Gl 441.

Description: Very large EB IV/MB I settlement with round circles and enclosures in the Ṣin valley near the confluence of *Naḥal Ṣin (Wādi al-Marra)* and *Naḥal Dārok̲ (Wādi al-Maharug*)*.

¶ Glueck, BASOR 159, 1960, 8.

---

*Transcription? Here following PEF 1:250.000 map.

1302.04 P.g. 1397.0275*

Name: Gl 436.

Description: Very small EB IV/MB I site. (burials?).

¶ Glueck, BASOR 159, 1960, 11.

1302.05 P.g. 1374.0268

Name: Gl 440.

Description: EB IV/MB I settlement in the Ṣin valley ca. 1/2 km S of *Naḥal Ṣin (Wādi al-Marra)*.

¶ Glueck, BASOR 159, 1960, 10.

1302.06 P.g. 1382.0267

Name: Gl 439.

Description: EB IV/MB I settlement in the Ṣin valley along the S bank of *Naḥal Ṣin (Wādi al-Marra)*.

¶ Glueck, BASOR 159, 1960, 10; Isr. Gen. Archives: IDA.

1302.07 P.g. 1393.0268

Name: Gl 436A.

Description: Very small EB IV/MB I site near *Naḥal Ṣin (Wādi al-Marra)*. (burials?).

¶ Glueck, BASOR 159, 1960, 11.

1302.08 P.g. 1391.0267

Name: Gl 437.

Description: EB IV/MB I settlement with much pottery along *Naḥal Ṣin (Wādi al-Marra)*.

¶ Glueck, BASOR 159, 1960, 10; Isr. Gen. Archives: IDA.

1302.09 P.g. 13250.02515

Name: None.

---

*The field map ref.: 1283.0208 (Cf. Thompson, ZDPV 91, 1975, in press) is, in this case, obviously an error.

0501.01

(1302.09)

Description: EB IV/MB I (?) settlement to the E of *ʿEn ʿȦqẹv (ʿAin Umm Kaʿb)* and *Naḥal ʿȦqẹv (Wādi Umm Kaʿb).*

¶ Isr. Gen. Archives: IDA.

0501.01 P.g. 053.017

Name: None.

Description: EB IV/MB I settlement with 3 tumuli along the *Wādi al-Mašāš.*

¶ Margovsky, Survey of North Sinai; Survey of Israel: IDA.

0501.02 P.g. ca. 054.015

Name: None.

Description: 3 separate EB IV/MB I findspots along the *Wādi Abū Sayyāl.*

¶ Margovsky, Survey of North Sinai: IDA.

0501.03 P.g. 0520.0143

Name: None.

Description: Very large EB IV/MB I settlement (ca. 200 x 300m) on *Ǧ. Halāl*, between *Wādi Umm-Saranīq* and *Wādi Abū Sayyāl.*

¶ Margovsky, Survey of North Sinai; Survey of Israel: IDA.

0501.04 P.g. 0503-11.0125-35

Name: None.

Description: EB IV/MB I tumuli found over large area E of *Wādi Umm Saranīq.*

¶ Margovsky, Survey of North Sinai; Survey of Israel: IDA.

0501.05 P.g. 051.013

Name: None.

Description: Scattered remains with EB IV/MB I pottery and tumuli

(0501.05)

N of *Ǧ. Halāl.*

¶ Margovsky, Survey of North Sinai: IDA.

0501.06 P.g. 0500.0124

Name: None.

Description: EB IV/MB I settlement with stone circles but little pottery N of *Ǧ. Halāl* along *Wādi Umm Sarānīq*.

¶ Margovsky, Survey of North Sinai: IDA.

0501.07 P.g. 0501.0123

Name: None.

Description: Small settlement (12 x 16m) with EB IV/MB I pottery and flints N of *Ǧ. Halāl* along the *Wādi Umm Sarānīq*.

¶ Margovsky, Survey of North Sinai; Survey of Israel: IDA.

0501.08 P.g. 0502.0124

Name: None.

Description: 2 stone circles with scattered flints and pottery from EB IV/MB I near *Wādi Umm Sarānīq*, N of *Ǧ. Halāl*.

¶ Margovsky, Survey of North Sinai; Survey of Israel: IDA.

0501.09 P.g. 0532.0115

Name: None.

Description: Very large area (ca. 400 x 400m) with EB IV/MB I pottery and tumuli N of *Ǧ. Halāl*.

¶ Margovsky, Survey of North Sinai; Survey of Israel: IDA.

0801.01 P.g. ca. 0855.0100

Name: *Muwēliḥ*.

Description: Scattered remains with EB IV/MB I pottery near the juncture of *Wādi Muwēliḥ* and *Wādi al-Abyaḍ*.

¶ Rothenberg, Sfunot Negev, 102.

0801.02 P.g. ca. 0868.0103

Name: None.

Description: Scattered remains with EB IV/MB I pottery along *Wādi Muwēliḥ* - *Wādi Ṣabḥa* ca. 3km NW of *ʿAin Quṣēma*.

¶ Rothenberg, Sfunot Negev, 102.

0901.01 P.g. 09985.01995

Name: Gl 340.

Description: EB IV/MB I settlement along the *Naḥal Bəẹrotayim (Wādi Birēn)*.

¶ Glueck, BASOR 145, 1957, 19n33; Survey of Negev: IDA.

0901.02 P.g. 0996.0192

Name: Gl 331a.

Description: EB IV/MB I settlement W of *Naḥal Bəẹrotayim (Wādi Birēn)*.

¶ Glueck, BASOR 145, 1957, 19n33; Survey of Negev: IDA.

0901.03 P.g. 0993.0177

Name: Gl 339.

Description: Very large EB IV/MB I settlement with very many stone circles and enclosures W of *Naḥal Bəẹrotayim (Wādi Birēn)*.

¶ Glueck, BASOR 145, 1957, 19n33; Rothenberg, Sfunot Negev, 102; Isr. Gen. Archives: IDA.

1001.01 P.g. 10470.01755

Name: Gl 346.

Description: Large EB IV/MB I settlement with much pottery on hill E of *Naḥal Horšȧ (Wādi Ḫurāša)* with tumuli and cairns. Glueck suggests that it is a large necropolis.

¶ Glueck, BASOR 145, 1957, 20; idem, BASOR 149, 1958, 10ff; idem, BASOR 152, 1958, 21-25; idem, BASOR 159, 1960, 3f; Rothenberg, Sfunot Negev, 104; Survey of Negev: IDA.

1001.02 P.g. 1084.0167

Name: None.

(1001.02)

Description: Small EB IV/MB I settlement ca. 1km to the W of *Naḥal Niṣȧnȧ (Wādi al-Ḥafīr)*.

¶ Isr. Gen. Archives: IDA.

1001.03 P.g. 1099.0142

Name: None.

Description: EB IV/MB I settlement with round circles along W bank of *Naḥal Niṣȧnȧ (Wādi al-Ḥafīr)*.

¶ Survey of Negev: IDA.

1001.04 P.g. 1022.0137

Name: Gl 343.

Description: EB IV/MB I settlement on slopes of *Har ʿĔzuz* above and E of *Naḥal ʿĔzuz (Wādi ʿUzēz)*.

¶ Glueck, BASOR 145, 1957, 19n33; Rothenberg, Sfunot Negev, 102; Survey of Negev: IDA.

1001.05 P.g. 1049.0105

Name: None.

Description: EB IV/MB I settlement on small hill immediately N of *Naḥal Mitgȧn (Wādi Ḫurāša)* and ca. 1/2km W of juncture of *Naḥal Mitgȧn (Wādi Ḫurāša)* and *Naḥal Ḥoršȧ (Wādi Ḫurāša)*.

¶ Isr. Gen. Archives: IDA.

1001.06 P.g. 1046.0103

Name: None.

Description: EB IV/MB I settlement on slopes immediately N of *Naḥal Mitgȧn (Wādi Ḫurāša)*.

¶ Isr. Gen. Archives: IDA.

1001.07 P.g. 1056.0105

Name: None.

Description: EB IV/MB I settlement on *Naḥal Ḥoršȧ (Wādi Ḫurāša)*

(1001.07)

immediately N of the juncture with *Naḥal Mitqán (Wādi Ḫurāša)*.

¶ Rothenberg, Sfunot Negev, 102.

1101.01 P.g. 1171.0190

Name: RM 183.

Description: EB IV/MB I settlement with stone circles and other structures on *Rámat Maṭrẹd (al-Maṭrada)*.

¶ Aharoni, IEJ 10, 1960, 25.

1101.02 P.g. 11725.01890

Name: None.

Description: Scattered remains with EB IV/MB I pottery and stone circles on *Rámat Maṭrẹd (al-Maṭrada)*.

¶ Survey of Israel: IDA.

1101.03 P.g. 1189.0186

Name: RM 131.

Description: EB IV/MB I settlement with stone circles and other structures on *Rámat Maṭrẹd (al-Maṭrada)* near *Naḥal Maṭrẹd (Wādi al-Maṭrada)*.

¶ Aharoni, IEJ 10, 1960, 25.

1101.04 P.g. 1193.0185

Name: None.

Description: Scattered remains with EB IV/MB I pottery and stone circles on *Rámat Maṭrẹd (al-Maṭrada)* along *Naḥal Maṭred (Wādi al-Maṭrada)*.

¶ Survey of Israel: IDA.

1101.05 P.g. 1197.0182

Name: RM 135.

Description: EB IV/MB I settlement with stone circles and other structures along S side of *Naḥal Maṭrẹd (Wādi al-Maṭrada)*.

¶ Aharoni, IEJ 10, 1960, 25.

1101.06 P.g. 1177.0178

Name: RM 185.

Description: EB IV/MB I settlement with stone circles and other structures on *Rámat Maṭrẹd (al-Maṭrada)*.

¶ Aharoni, IEJ 10, 1960, 25.

1101.07 P.g. 11785.01770

Name: None.

Description: Scattered remains with EB IV/MB I pottery on *Rámat Maṭrẹd (al-Maṭrada)*.

¶ Survey of Israel: IDA.

1101.08 P.g. 11885.01715

Name: RM 137.

Description: Large EB IV/MB I settlement with stone circles and buildings on *Rámat Maṭrẹd (al-Maṭrada)* near tributary to *Naḥal Maṭrẹd (Wadi al-Maṭrada)*.

¶ Aharoni, IEJ 10, 1960, 25; Survey of Israel: IDA.

1101.09 P.g. 1176.0167

Name: None.

Description: EB IV/MB I remains with 3 tumuli on *Rámat Maṭrẹd (al-Maṭrada)* near small tributary of *Naḥal La'ănȧ (Wādi Qatun*)*.

¶ Survey of Israel: IDA.

1101.10 P.g. 1178.0167

Name: RM 186.

Description: EB IV/MB I settlement with stone circles and other structures on *Rámat Maṭrẹd (al-Maṭrada)* near small tributary of *Naḥal La'ănȧ (Wādi Qatun*)*.

¶ Aharoni, IEJ 10, 1960, 25.

---

*Transcription? Here following PEF 1:250.000 map.

1101.11 P.g. 1183.0159

Name: None.

Description: Small EB IV/MB I settlement with little pottery on *Rámat Maṭrẹd (al-Maṭrada).*

¶ Isr. Gen. Archives: IDA.

1101.12 P.g. 1184.0157

Name: None.

Description: Scattered remains with EB IV/MB I pottery on *Rámat Maṭrẹd (al-Maṭrada).*

¶ Isr. Gen. Archives: IDA.

1101.13 P.g. 1196.0154

Name: None.

Description: EB IV/MB I settlement on *Naḥal ʿȦvdat (Wādi ʿAbda).*

¶ Survey of Negev: IDA.

1101.14 P.g. 1197.0143

Name: RM 167.

Description: EB IV/MB I settlement with stone circles and other structures on *Naḥal ʿȦvdat (Wādi ʿAbda).*

¶ Aharoni, IEJ 10, 1960, 25.

1101.15 P.g. 1199.0140

Name: RM 166.

Description: EB IV/MB I settlement with stone circles and buildings along upper reaches of *Naḥal ʿȦvdat (Wādi ʿAbda).*

¶ Aharoni, IEJ 10, 1960, 25.

1101.16 P.g. 1175.0136

Name: Gl 410.

Description: EB IV/MB I settlement with much pottery and flints

(1101.16)

on slopes near *Naḥal La^cănȧ (Wādi Qatun*)*.

¶ Glueck, BASOR 152, 1958, 32; Had. Arch., 1964, 20; Survey of Negev: IDA.

1101.17 P.g. 1187.0138

Name: None.

Description: EB IV/MB I settlement with stone circles between *Naḥal ʿȦvdat (Wādi ʿAbda)* and *Naḥal Laʿănȃ (Wādi Qatun*)*.

¶ Survey of Israel: IDA.

1201.01 P.g. 1201.0196

Name: RM 115.

Description: EB IV/MB I settlement with round circles and buildings on *Ramat Maṭreḍ (al-Maṭrada)* ca. 400m W of *Naḥal Maṭreḍ (Wādi al Maṭrada)*.

¶ Aharoni, IEJ 10, 1960, 25.

1201.02 P.g. 12015.01950

Name: None.

Description: Small settlement with EB IV/MB I pottery on *Ramat Maṭreḍ (al-Maṭrada)* on W bank of *Naḥal Maṭreḍ (Wādi al-Maṭrada)*.

¶ Survey of Israel: IDA.

1201.03 P.g. 12042.01942

Name: None.

Description: Scattered remains with EB IV/MB I pottery on *Naḥal Maṭreḍ (Wādi al-Maṭrada)*.

¶ Survey of Negev: IDA.

1201.04 P.g. 12052.01931

Name: None.

Description: Scattered remains with EB IV/MB I pottery over area

---

* Transcription? Here following PEF 1:250.000 map.

(1201.04)

(ca. 25 x 12m) on *Naḥal Maṭrẹd (Wādi al-Maṭrada)*.

¶ Survey of Israel: IDA.

1201.05 P.g. 1205.0191

Name: RM 160.

Description: EB IV/MB I settlement with round circles and buildings on *Ràmat Maṭrẹd (al-Maṭrada)* along *Naḥal Maṭrẹd (Wādi al-Maṭrada)*.

¶ Aharoni, IEJ 10, 1960, 25.

1201.06 P.g. 1211.0192

Name: RM 127.

Description: EB IV/MB I settlement with stone circles and tumuli ca. 1/2km E of *Naḥal Maṭrẹd (Wādi al-Maṭrada)*.

¶ Aharoni, IEJ 10, 1960, 25; Survey of Israel: IDA.

1201.07 P.g. 12095.01890

Name: None.

Description: EB IV/MB I settlement with stone circles, much pottery and tumuli N and E of *Naḥal Maṭrẹd (Wādi al-Maṭrada)*. EB IV/MB I pottery also found at coordinates 12090.01895.

¶ Survey of Israel: IDA.

1201.08 P.g. 12005.01810

Name: None.

Description: Scattered remains with EB IV/MB I pottery and 2 stone round enclosures on tributary of *Naḥal Maṭrẹd (Wādi al-Maṭrada)*.

¶ Survey of Israel: IDA.

1201.09 P.g. 1201.0182

Name: RM 134.

Description: Scattered remains with EB IV/MB I pottery, tumuli and stone enclosures on S side of *Naḥal Maṭrẹd (Wādi al-Maṭrada*

¶ Aharoni, IEJ 10, 1960, 25.

1201.10 P.g. 1205.0181

Name: None.

Description: 2 stone circles with pottery (EB IV/MB I?) on tributary to *Naḥal Maṭreḍ (Wādi al-Maṭrada)*.

¶ Survey of Israel: IDA.

1201.11 P.g. 1206.0181

Name: RM 133.

Description: EB IV/MB I settlement with stone circles and buildings near *Naḥal Maṭreḍ (Wādi al-Maṭrada)*.

¶ Aharoni, IEJ 10, 1960, 25.

1201.12 P.g. 12095.01805

Name: None.

Description: EB IV/MB I settlement with stone circles on *Naḥal Maṭreḍ (Wādi al-Maṭrada)*.

¶ Survey of Negev: IDA.

1201.13 P.g. 1203.0179

Name: RM 173.

Description: Scattered remains with EB IV/MB I pottery, tumuli and stone enclosures near tributary to *Naḥal Maṭreḍ (Wādi al-Maṭrada)*.

¶ Aharoni, IEJ 10, 1960, 25.

1201.14 P.g. 1214.0177

Name: None.

Description: Tumuli with EB IV/MB I pottery along bank of *Naḥal Maṭreḍ (Wādi al-Maṭrada)*.

¶ Survey of Israel: IDA.

1201.15 P.g. 1212.0175

Name: RM 174.

Description: Scattered remains with EB IV/MB I pottery, tumuli and stone enclosures along bank of *Naḥal Maṭreḍ (Wādi al-Maṭrada)*.

(1201.15)

¶ Aharoni, IEJ 10, 1960, 25.

1201.16 P.g. 12135.01740

Name: None.

Description: Tumuli with EB IV/MB I pottery near tributary to *Naḥal Maṭrẹd (Wādi al-Maṭrada).*

¶ Survey of Israel: IDA.

1201.17 P.g. 12190.01750

Name: RM 171.

Description: Scattered remains with EB IV/MB I pottery, tumuli and large stone enclosure near NW bank of *Naḥal ᶜȦvdat (Wādi ᶜAbda).*

¶ Aharoni, IEJ 10, 1960, 25; Survey of Israel: IDA.

1201.18 P.g. 1207.0155

Name: RM 168.

Description: EB IV/MB I settlement with stone circles and buildings along SE bank of *Naḥal ᶜȦvdat (Wādi ᶜAbda).*

¶ Aharoni, IEJ 10, 1960, 25; Survey of Negev: IDA.

1201.19 P.g. 1291.0123

Name: None.

Description: Scattered remains with EB IV/MB I pottery on slopes of hill just SW of *Naḥal Ṣin (Wādi an-Nafḫ).*

¶ Isr. Gen. Archives: IDA.

1201.20 P.g. 1284.0118

Name: None.

Description: EB IV/MB I settlement on slopes along E bank of *Naḥal Ṣin (Wādi an-Nafḫ).*

¶ Isr. Gen. Archives: IDA.

1301.01 P.g. 13220.01585

Name: None.

Description: Scattered remains with EB IV/MB I pottery over small area on E bank of *Naḥal Ṣin (Wādi an-Nafḫ)*.

¶ Isr. Gen. Archives: IDA.

1301.02 P.g. 13795.01570

Name: Gl 133.

Description: EB settlement on tributary to *Naḥal Gərȧfon (Wādi Mušēša aš-Šarqīya)*.

¶ Glueck, BASOR 138, 1955, 12; Isr. Gen. Archives: IDA.

1301.03 P.g. 1389.0146

Name: Gl 132c*.

Description: EB settlement on tributary to *Naḥal Gərȧfon (Wādi Mušēša aš-Šarqīya)*.

¶ Glueck, BASOR 138, 1955, 12; Isr. Gen. Archives: IDA.

1401.01 P.g. 1406.0147

Name: Gl 182.

Description: EB settlement along S bank of *Naḥal Maḥmȧl (Wādi Ramān)*.

¶ Glueck, BASOR 138, 1955, 12; Isr. Gen. Archives: IDA.

1501.01 P.g. 1587.0124

Name: Gl 452.

Description: Very large EB IV/MB I settlement (ca. 400 x 100m) N of *Naḥal Marzeṿȧ (Wādi Mirzaba)*.

¶ Glueck, BA 22, 1959, 85-87; idem, BASOR 159, 1960, 8-12; Isr. Gen. Archives: IDA.

---

* Published reference is to "132e" (sic!); however, field map shows 132a, b, c only.

0900.01 P.g. 0908.0080

Name: None.

Description: EB IV/MB I settlement between *ʿAin Quṣēma* ca. 1km to the W and *Wādi ʿAin* to the E.

¶ Rothenberg, Sfunot Negev, 102.

0900.02 P.g. 0970.0088

Name: None.

Description: Scattered remains with EB IV/MB I pottery on *Ǧ. al-ʿAin* ca. 2 1/2km ENE of *ʿAin al-Qudērāt*.

¶ Rothenberg, Sfunot Negev, 102.

0900.03 P.g. ca. 0915.0070

Name: None.

Description: Scattered remains with EB IV/MB I pottery near *Wādi ʿAin* above and 2km SE of *ʿAin Quṣēma*.

¶ Rothenberg, Sfunot Negev, 102.

0900.04 P.g. 0924.0075

Name: None.

Description: EB IV/MB I settlement on slopes of *Ǧ. al-ʿAin* near *Wādi ʿAin*.

¶ Rothenberg, Sfunot Negev, 102.

0900.05 P.g. 0937.0077

Name: None.

Description: Scattered remains with EB IV/MB I pottery on slopes of *Ǧ. al-ʿAin* ca. 2 1/2km WNW of *ʿAin al-Qudērāt*.

¶ Rothenberg, Sfunot Negev, 102.

0900.06 P.g. 0960.0070

Name: None.

Description: EB IV/MB I settlement N of *Wādi al-Qudērāt* ca. 800m N of *ʿAin al-Qudērāt*.

¶ Rothenberg, Sfunot Negev, 102.

0900.07 P.g. 0971.0075

Name: None.

Description: EB IV/MB I settlement on N side of *Wādi al-Qudērāt*.

¶ Rothenberg, Sfunot Negev, 102.

0900.08 P.g. 0925.0065

Name: None.

Description: EB IV/MB I settlement near *Wādi ʿAin - Wādi Umm Hāšim*.

¶ Rothenberg, Sfunot Negev, 102.

0900.09 P.g. 0955.0069

Name: None.

Description: EB IV/MB I settlement on *Ǧ. al-ʿAin*, above *ʿAin al-Qudērāt*.

¶ Rothenberg, Sfunot Negev, 102.

0900.10 P.g. 0962.0068

Name: None.

Description: Scattered remains with EB IV/MB I pottery about 6-700m ENE of *ʿAin al-Qudērāt*.

¶ Rothenberg, Sfunot Negev, 102.

0900.10A P.g. 0964.0064

Name: Roth 306 .

Description: Scattered remains with possibly EB IV/MB I pottery near the oasis of *ʿAin al-Qudērāt*.

¶ Courtesy of B. Rothenberg.

0900.11 P.g. 0960.0062

Name: *ʿAin al-Qudērāt*.

Description: Scattered remains with EB IV/MB I pottery at the oasis of *ʿAin al-Qudērāt*.

¶ Albright, BASOR 163, 1961, 37; Dothan, IEJ 15, 1965, 134; Rothenberg, Sfunot Negev, 102; Survey of Israel: IDA.

0900.12 P.g. 0956.0057

Name: None.

Description: Scattered remains with EB IV/MB I pottery N of *Wādi Umm Hāšim*.

¶ Rothenberg, Sfunot Negev, 102.

0900.13 P.g. 0982.0055 (Glueck's field map ref.: 09815.00525)

Name: None.

Description: Scattered remains with EB IV/MB I pottery ca. 2 1/4km ESE of *ʿAin al-Qudērāt*.

¶ Rothenberg, Sfunot Negev, 102; Thompson, ZDPV 91, 1975, in press.

0900.14 P.g. 0930.0041

Name: None.

Description: EB IV/MB I settlement in mountains S of *Wādi Umm Hāšim*.

¶ Rothenberg, Sfunot Negev, 102.

0900.15 P.g. 0951.0042

Name: None.

Description: Scattered remains with EB IV/MB I pottery on S side of *Wādi Umm Hāšim*, ca. 2km SSW of *ʿAin al-Qudērāt*.

¶ Rothenberg, Sfunot Negev, 102.

0900.16 P.g. 0955.0034

Name: None.

Description: Scattered remains with EB IV/MB I pottery on tributary of *Wādi Umm Hāšim*.

¶ Rothenberg, Sfunot Negev, 102.

0900.17 P.g. 0990.0021

Name: None.

Description: Scattered remains with EB IV/MB I pottery ca. 3km NNW of *ʿAin Qudēs*.

¶ Rothenberg, Sfunot Negev, 102.

0900.18 P.g. 0984.0009

Name: None.

Description: Scattered remains with EB IV/MB I pottery ca. 3km NW of *ᶜAin Qudēs*.

¶ Rothenberg, Sfunot Negev, 102.

1000.01 P.g. 1023.0098

Name: None.

Description: Scattered remains with EB IV/MB I pottery ca. 1km NW of *Naḥal Mitgȧn (Wādi Ḫurāšа)*.

¶ Rothenberg, Sfunot Negev, 102.

1000.02 P.g. 1039.0095

Name: Roth 102.

Description: Scattered remains with LB/EI pottery.

¶ Courtesy of B. Rothenberg.

1000.03 P.g. 1042.0097

Name: None.

Description: Scattered remains with EB IV/MB I pottery on *Naḥal Mitgȧn (Wādi Ḫurāša)*.

¶ Rothenberg, Sfunot Negev, 102.

1000.04 P.g. 1007.0075

Name: None.

Description: Scattered remains with EB IV/MB I pottery on tributary to *Wādi al-ᶜAsalī, Wādi al-Qudērāt*.

¶ Rothenberg, Sfunot Negev, 102.

1000.05 P.g. 1038.0072

Name: Roth 103.

Description: Scattered remains with possibly LB/EI pottery.

¶ Courtesy of B. Rothenberg.

1000.06 P.g. 1061.0076

Name: Gl 421.

Description: Large EB IV/MB I settlement on hill between *Naḥal Ḥoršå (Wādi Ḫurāša)* and *Naḥal Ḥåsni (Wādi al-Ḥafīr)*.

¶ Glueck, BASOR 159, 1960, 5; Isr. Gen. Archives: IDA.

1000.07 P.g. 1056.0054

Name: Roth 108A.

Description: Scattered remains with LB/EI pottery.

¶ Courtesy of B. Rothenberg.

1000.08 P.g. 1075.0054

Name: Roth 110.

Description: EB IV/MB I settlement with stone circles and much pottery (some from LB/EI) between *Naḥal Ḥoršå (Wādi Ḫurāša)* and *Naḥal Ḥåsni (Wādi al-Ḫafīr)*.

¶ Sfunot Negev, 79; further, courtesy of B. Rothenberg.

1000.09 P.g. 1043.0036

Name: Gl 424 (identical to or near Roth 104: P.g. 1043.0035).

Description: EB IV/MB I settlement near *ʿAin Qudēs* along *Naḥal Qådeš Barneʿa (Wādi al-Qudērāt)*; some possibly LB/EI pottery at Roth 104.

¶ Glueck, BASOR 159, 1960, 6; further, courtesy of B. Rothenberg.

1000.10 P.g. 1053.0033

Name: Roth 109.

Description: Large EB IV/MB I settlement with stone circles and much pottery along *Naḥal Qådeš Barneʿa (Wādi al-Qudērāt)*.

¶ Rothenberg, Sfunot Negev, 78.

1000.11 P.g. 1053.0030

Name: None.

Description: Scattered remains with EB IV/MB I pottery along *Naḥal Qådeš Barneʿa (Wādi al-Qudērāt)*.

(1000.11)

¶ Rothenberg, Sfunot Negev, 102.

1000.12 P.g. 1015.0028

Name: None.

Description: Scattered remains with EB IV/MB I pottery and stone circles along S bank of *Wādi al-Huwar*.

¶ Survey of Israel: IDA.

1000.13 P.g. 1016.0025

Name: None.

Description: Scattered remains with EB IV/MB I pottery along N bank of the *Wādi Umm Hāšim*.

¶ Rothenberg, Sfunot Negev, 102.

1200.01 P.g. 1274.0099

Name: Gl 349.

Description: EB IV/MB I settlement with much pottery near juncture of several small wādis with *Naḥal Ṣin (Wādi an-Nafḫ)*.

¶ Glueck, BASOR 145, 1957, 17; Survey of Negev: IDA.

1200.02 P.g. 12530.00315

Name: Gl 149c.

Description: Very large EB IV/MB I settlement ca. 1km NW of *Naḥal Ṣin (Wādi an-Nafḫ)*.

¶ Glueck, BASOR 138, 1955, 25; Isr. Gen. Archives: IDA.

1200.03 P.g. 1262.0037

Name: RM 22.

Description: Small EB IV/MB I settlement with about 10 stone circles ca. 1/2km W of *Naḥal Ṣin (Wādi an-Nafḫ)*.

¶ Aharoni, IEJ 8, 1958, 248.

1200.04 P.g. 1298.0022

Name: None.

Description: Scattered remains with EB IV/MB I pottery ca. 1km W of *Miṣpe Rámon* near tributary wādi to *Naḥal Ṣin (Wādi an-Nafḫ)*.

¶ Isr. Gen. Archives: IDA.

1200.05 P.g. 1234.0019*

Name: Gl 152.

Description: Scattered remains with EB IV/MB I pottery ca. 1km N of *Naḥal Ṣin (Wādi an-Nafḫ)*.

¶ Glueck, BASOR 138, 1955, 25; Isr. Gen. Archives: IDA.

1200.06 P.g. 1239.0017

Name: Gl 147b.

Description: Scattered remains with EB IV/MB I pottery along W bank of *Naḥal Ṣin (Wādi an-Nafḫ)*.

¶ Glueck, BASOR 138, 1955, 24f.

1200.07 P.g. 1242.0017

Name: Gl 147a.

Description: Scattered remains with EB IV/MB I pottery ca. 1/2km NNW of *Naḥal Ṣin (Wādi an-Nafḫ)*.

¶ Glueck, BASOR 138, 1955, 24f.

1200.08 P.g. 1247.0018

Name: Gl 147.

Description: EB IV/MB I settlement with much pottery on flat ridge along W bank of *Naḥal Ṣin (Wādi an-Nafḫ)*.

¶ Glueck, BASOR 132, 1952, 33; idem, BASOR 138, 1955, 24f; Isr. Gen. Archives: IDA.

---

* Glueck's published map coordinates for this site, in contrast to those for 147. 147A and 147B, seem preferable to the coordinates from his field map (1232.0014) since the site is described as north - not south - of site 147.

1300.01 P.g. 1325.0086

Name: None.

Description: EB IV/MB I settlement with stone circles on hill ca. 1/2km N of *Naḥal Ḥawwȧ (Wādi al-Ḥawwā)*.

¶ Survey of Israel: IDA.

1300.02 P.g. 1325.0063

Name: RM 45.

Description: Large EB IV/MB I settlement with stone circles, buildings and much pottery near *Naḥal Ḥawwȧ (Wādi al-Ḥawwā)*.

¶ Aharoni, IEJ 8, 1958, 248.

1300.03 P.g. 1325.0065

Name: RM 15.

Description: Small EB IV/MB I settlement with stone circles on ridge opposite 1300.02.

¶ Aharoni, IEJ 8, 1958, 248. 256; Survey of Israel: IDA.

1300.04 P.g. 1326.0058

Name: None.

Description: Remains of EB IV/MB I settlement found in cave in *Naḥal Ḥawwȧ (Wādi al-Ḥawwā)*.

¶ Isr. Gen. Archives: IDA.

1600.01 P.g. 1666.0046

Name: Roth 57.

Description: EB IV/MB I settlement with much pottery (some from LB/EI) found at *ᶜEn Raḥel*.

¶ Rothenberg, Sfunot Negev, 127; further, courtesy of B. Rothenberg.

1600.02 P.g. ca. 166.004

Name: Roth 57A.

Description: LB/EI settlement with much pottery near spring not far from 1600.01.

1800.01

(1600.02)

¶ Rothenberg, Sfunot Negev, 127; further, courtesy of B. Rothenberg.

1800.01 P.g. 1805.0050

Name: Roth 56B.

Description: EB IV/MB I settlement with stone circles and many tombs.

¶ Rothenberg, Sfunot Negev, 122f.

1900.01 P.g. 1972.0042

Name: Gl II 14; *Fēnān*.

Description: Very large EB IV/MB I copper smelting site on N side of *Wādi al-Ġuwēr* and on both sides of *Wādi aš-Šeqer**.

¶ Glueck, EEP II, 33; Robinson, AJA 39, 1935, 120.

0499.01 P.g. 0432.9933

Name: Roth 674.

Description: Small settlement with stone enclosures along narrow wādi ca. 1km SE of spring; some flints possibly from Chalcolithic-EB I.

¶ Courtesy of B. Rothenberg.

1099.01 P.g. 10065.99925

Name: None.

Description: EB IV/MB I settlement along *Wādi Qudēs* near *ʿAin Qudēs*.

¶ Glueck, BASOR 179, 1965, 12.

1099.02 P.g. 1046.9925

Name: Gl 476.

Description: EB IV/MB I settlement in hills near *Har Ḥarif (Rās Ḫarūf)* ca. 3/4km SW of *Naḥal Ḥarif (Wādi Ḫarūf)*.

---

* Transcription? Here following PEF 1:250.000 map.

(1099.02)

¶ Glueck, BASOR 179, 1965, 10.

1099.03 P.g. 10835.99040

Name: None.

Description: Flints from EB IV/MB I (?) over small area (840m^2) on hill above *Naḥal Ḥoršȧ (Wādi Ḫurāša)*.

¶ Southern Methodist University Expedition to the Negev; Isr. Gen. Archives: IDA.

1099.04 P.g. 1080.9900

Name: None.

Description: Scattered remains with EB IV/MB I pottery on *Har Ḥȧrif (Rās Ḫarūf)*.

¶ Isr. Gen. Archives: IDA.

1099.05 P.g. 1099.9907

Name: RM 31.

Description: Scattered remains with EB IV/MB I pottery on slopes of *Har Romẹm (Rās al-Ḫurāša)* above *Naḥal ʾẸlonim (Wādi Luṣṣān)*.

¶ Aharoni, IEJ 8, 1958, 249.

1099.06 P.g. 1095.9904

Name: Gl 474.

Description: Small EB IV/MB I settlement on slopes of *Har Romẹm (Rās al-Ḫurāša)* ca. 1km NW of *Naḥal ʾẸlonim (Wādi Luṣṣān)*.

¶ Glueck, BASOR 179, 1965, 10.

1199.01 P.g. 1160.9950

Name: None.

Description: EB IV/MB I settlement with stone circles along *Naḥal Niṣȧnȧ (Wādi al-Aǧram)*.

¶ Aharoni, IEJ 8, 1958, 249.

1199.02 P.g. 1159.9943

Name: RM 39.

Description: Very large EB IV/MB I settlement with stone circles on slopes along *Naḥal Niṣànà (Wādi al-Ağram)*.

¶ Aharoni, IEJ 8, 1958, 249.

1199.03 P.g. 111.993

Name: RM 33.

Description: Scattered remains with EB IV/MB I pottery and stone circles near *Naḥal ᵓẸlot (Wādi Ḫurāša)*.

¶ Aharoni, IEJ 8, 1958, 249.

1199.04 P.g. 1123.9934

Name: None.

Description: Scattered remains with EB IV/MB I pottery along *Naḥal ᵓẸlot (Wādi Ḫurāša)*.

¶ Survey of Israel: IDA.

1199.05 P.g. 111.992

Name: None.

Description: Small EB IV/MB I settlement with stone circles near *Naḥal ᵓẸlot (Wādi Ḫurāša)*.

¶ Aharoni, IEJ 8, 1958, 249.

1199.06 P.g. 1131.9924

Name: None.

Description: EB IV/MB I settlement with stone circles along *Naḥal ᵓẸlot (Wādi Ḫurāša)*.

¶ Survey of Israel: IDA.

1199.07 P.g. 1106.9911

Name: None.

Description: Scattered remains with EB IV/MB I pottery and stone circles on *Har Romẹm (Rās al-Ḫurāša)*.

¶ Survey of Israel: IDA.

1199.08 P.g. 11015.99100

Name: None.

Description: Scattered remains with EB IV/MB I pottery on *Har Romem (Rās al-Ḫurāša)*.

¶ Aharoni, IEJ 8, 1958, 249.

1199.09 P.g. 1101.9909

Name: None.

Description: Small EB IV/MB I settlement with stone circles on *Har Romem (Rās al-Ḫurāša)*.

¶ Isr. Gen. Archives: IDA.

1199.10 P.g. 1101.9906

Name: None.

Description: EB IV/MB I settlement with stone circles on *Har Romem (Rās al-Ḫurāša)*.

¶ Isr. Gen. Archives: IDA.

1199.11 P.g. 1102.9902

Name: RM 30; Gl 473.

Description: Large EB IV/MB I settlement with a series of stone circles and cairns and much pottery on *Har Romem (Rās al-Ḫurāša)*.

¶ Aharoni, IEJ 8, 1958, 249; Glueck, BASOR 179, 1965, 11; Survey of Israel: IDA.

1199.12 P.g. 1111.9908

Name: RM 38.

Description: Room or tower along "K-Line" (long EB IV/MB I wall).

¶ Aharoni, IEJ 8, 1958, 250.

1199.13 P.g. 1115.9902

Name: Gl 472.

Description: Scattered remains with EB IV/MB I pottery and a series of stone cairns.

(1199.13)

¶ Glueck, BASOR 179, 1965, 11.

1199.14 P.g. 1118.9907

Name: None.

Description: EB IV/MB I settlement on *Har Romem (Rās al-Ḫurāša)*.

¶ Isr. Gen. Archives: IDA.

1199.15 P.g. 1123.9905

Name: None.

Description: Scattered remains with EB IV/MB I pottery on *Har Romem (Rās al-Ḫurāša)*.

¶ Isr. Gen. Archives: IDA.

1199.16 P.g. 1132.9906

Name: None.

Description: EB IV/MB I settlement with stone circles on slopes of *Har Ramon (Rās ar-Ramān)*.

¶ Survey of Negev: IDA.

1199.17 P.g. 1138.9902

Name: None.

Description: Scattered remains with EB IV/MB I pottery on *Har Ramon (Rās ar-Ramān)*.

¶ Isr. Gen. Archives: IDA.

1199.18 P.g. 11480.99015

Name: RM 37*.

Description: Large EB IV/MB I cairn at E end of "K-line" on *Har Ramon (Rās ar-Ramān)*, cf. 1199.19.

¶ Aharoni, IEJ 8, 1958, 249; Isr. Gen. Archives; Survey of Israel: IDA.

---

* Not the same site as Gl 140.

1199.19 P.g. 1118.9907 to 1148.9901

Name: None.

Description: EB IV/MB I stone wall ("K-line") extending over 4kms between *Har Romem (Rās al-Ḫurāša)* and *Har Rȧmon (Rās ar-Ramān)*.

¶ Aharoni, IEJ 8, 1958, 237. 249; Isr. Gen. Archives: IDA.

1299.01 P.g. 1209.9999

Name: RM 24.

Description: EB IV/MB I settlement with stone circles along *Naḥal Niṣȧnȧ (Wādi al-Aǧram)*.

¶ Aharoni, IEJ 8, 1958, 249.

1299.02 P.g. 1259.9904

Name: Gl 234b.

Description: Isolated EB IV/MB I burial S of *Maḵteš Rȧmon (Wādi Ramān)*.

¶ Glueck, BASOR 142, 1956, 20f.

2099.01 P.g. 2020.9925

Name: None.

Description: Scattered remains with 1 clearly datable EB IV/MB I sherd near *ʿAin Niǧil* by the *Wādi Niǧil*.

¶ Glueck, EEP III, 53f. and 255.

1098.01 P.g. ca. 1075.9898

Name: None.

Description: EB IV/MB I structures on *Har Ḫȧrif (Ǧ. Ḫarūf)*.

¶ Southern Methodist University Expedition to the Negev, 1969; Isr. Gen. Archives: IDA.

1098.02 P.g. 1074.9894

Name: Gl 475.

Description: EB IV/MB I cemetery covering top and upper slopes of

(1098.02)

Har Ḥarif (Ǧ. Ḥarūf).

¶ Glueck, BASOR 179, 1965, 10, 12.

1098.03 P.g. 1070.9815.

Name: Gl 477.

Description: EB IV/MB I settlement with several burial cairns.

¶ Glueck, BASOR 179, 1965, 10.

1098.04 P.g. 1070.9810

Name: None.

Description: EB IV/MB I settlement with group of burial cairns ca. 3/4km N of *ʿEn Ha-Məʿārā (ʿAin Muġāra).*

¶ Glueck, BASOR 179, 1965, 11.

1098.05 P.g. 1069.9802

Name: Gl 471.

Description: EB IV/MB I settlement: *ʿEn Ha-Məʿārā (ʿAin Muġāra).*

¶ Glueck, BASOR 179, 1965, 6f.

1198.01 P.g. 1173.9842

Name: Gl 201.

Description: Very large EB IV/MB I settlement over several hills near the beginning of *Naḥal Bəroqā (Wādi Umm Brērig).*

¶ Glueck, BASOR 138, 1955, 27f; idem, BASOR 179, 1965, 10.

1198.02 P.g. 1198.9811

Name: Gl 203.

Description: EB IV/MB I settlement along *Naḥal Məāzẹr (Wādi Muʿēḏir).*

¶ Glueck, BASOR 179, 1965, 10.

1198.03 P.g. 1139.9806

Name: Gl 268.

Description: EB IV/MB I settlement N of tributary to *Naḥal Bəroqȧ (Wādi Umm Brērig).*

¶ Glueck, BASOR 142, 1956, 21; idem, BASOR 179, 1965, 10.

1298.01 P.g. 1222.9899

Name: Gl 200.

Description: Small EB IV/MB I settlement with ca. 5 stone circles on the *Naḥal ʿOreḍ (Wādi Umm Ṣāliḥ).*

¶ Glueck, BASOR 138, 1955, 28; idem, BASOR 142, 1956, 21; idem, BASOR 179, 1965, 10; Isr. Gen. Archives: IDA.

1298.02 P.g. 1244.9871

Name: None.

Description: EB IV/MB I settlement over several small hills along the *Naḥal ʿȦrod (Wādi al-ʿUdēd).*

¶ Isr. Gen. Archives: IDA.

1298.03 P.g. 1204.9854

Name: Gl 493.

Description: EB IV/MB I settlement on slopes of hills N of *Naḥal Qəṣiʿȧ (Wādi Qaṣā).*

¶ Glueck, BASOR 179, 1965, 10.

0997.01 P.g. 0905.9782

Name: Roth 307.

Description: Scattered remains with pottery and possibly flints from EB IV/MB I.

¶ Courtesy of B. Rothenberg.

1097.01 P.g. 1071.9797

Name: Gl 471a.

Description: Large EB IV/MB I settlement with stone circles on slopes of hill ca. 4-500m SE of *ᶜEn Ha-Məᶜȧrȧ (ᶜAin Muġāra)* and E above *Wādi Maqraᶜa.*

¶ Glueck, BASOR 179, 1965, 7.

1197.01 P.g. 1121.9791

Name: Gl 272.

Description: EB IV/MB I settlement on tributary to *Naḥal Batur (Wādi al-Māyēn).*

¶ Glueck, BASOR 179, 1965, 10.

1297.01 P.g. 1243.9796

Name: Gl 483.

Description: Large EB IV/MB I settlement with stone circles overlooking *Naḥal Maᶜṣẹr (Wādi Muᶜēḏir).*

¶ Glueck, BASOR 179, 1965, 14.

1297.02 P.g. 12185.97560

Name: Gl 484.

Description: Small EB IV/MB I settlement with little pottery on *Naḥal Yafruq (Wādi Aǧramīya).*

¶ Glueck, BASOR 179, 1965, 14.

1297.03 P.g. 1237.9738

Name: Gl 485.

Description: Very large EB IV/MB I settlement overlooking junction of *Naḥal Karkom (Wādi al-ᶜUdēd)* and *Naḥal Gešur (Wādi al-ᶜUdēd).*

¶ Glueck, BASOR 179, 1965, 13.

1297.04 P.g. ca. 1237.9732

Name: Gl 485.

Description: EB IV/MB I burial cairns on N slope of hill.

(1297.04)

¶ Glueck, BASOR 179, 1965, 13.

1297.05 P.g. ca. 1238.9728

Name: Gl 485.

Description: EB IV/MB I settlement on hilltop overlooking *Bə ẹr Karkom (Bīr ᶜUdēd)*.

¶ Glueck, BASOR 179, 1965, 13.

1397.01 P.g. 1380.9736

Name: Gl 481a.

Description: Small EB IV/MB I settlement with much pottery - also burials - on N side of *Naḥal Karkom (Wadi al-Ubara*)*.

¶ Glueck, BASOR 179, 1965, 15.

1997.01 P.g. 1918.9710

Name: Petra.

Description: EB settlement at Petra near the *Wādi Mūsā*.

¶ Mandate Archives, Pal. Museum: IDA.

9696.01 P.g. 9635.9604

Name: Roth 580.

Description: Scattered remains with many tumuli. Flints from either the Proto- or Early Dynastic periods and some possibly EB IV/MB I pottery.

¶ Courtesy of B. Rothenberg.

9495.01 P.g. 9499.9575

Name: Roth 578.

Description: Scattered remains with some possibly Chalcolithic-EB I and EB IV/MB I pottery.

¶ Courtesy of B. Rothenberg.

---

* Transcription? Here following PEF 1:250.000 map.

9495.02 P.g. 9433.9564

Name: Roth 579.

Description: Scattered remains with one large tumulus and possibly Chalcolithic-EB I and EB IV/MB I pottery.

¶ Courtesy of B. Rothenberg.

9695.01 P.g. 9627.9598

Name: Roth 581.

Description: Large EB IV/MB I settlement with much pottery, stone circles and rooms and 1 tumulus. Some flints and pottery are possibly Chalcolithic-EB I.

¶ Courtesy of B. Rothenberg.

0995.01 P.g. 0945.9558

Name: Roth 309.

Description: Scattered remains with some possibly LB/EI pottery.

¶ Courtesy of B. Rothenberg.

9694.01 P.g. 9686.9433

Name: Roth 554A.

Description: Small structure and attached tumuli with pottery and flints from Chalcolithic-EB I.

¶ Courtesy of B. Rothenberg.

9694.02 P.g. 9687.9430

Name: Roth 554.

Description: Stone circle with many tumuli over 100m area. Pottery and flints possibly from EB IV/MB I and flints from either the Proto- or Early Dynastic periods.

¶ Courtesy of B. Rothenberg.

9794.01 P.g. 9723.9425 E.g. 31° 8227.8184

Name: None.

Description: EB IV/MB I settlement with stone circles on tributary

(9794.01)

of the *Wādi al-Ġēdara* with terraced wādi about 300m S of site.

¶ Rothenberg, God's Wilderness, 61.

9794.02 P.g. 9728.9423 E.g. 31° 8231.81835

Name: None.

Description: Small EB IV/MB I settlement with stone circles on tributary to *Wādi al-Ġēdara*.

¶ Rothenberg, God's Wilderness, 61.

9794.03 P.g. 9730.9425 E.g. 31° 8232.8185

Name: None.

Description: Small EB IV/MB I settlement with stone circles along tributary to *Wādi al-Ġēdara*.

¶ Rothenberg, God's Wilderness, 61.

9794.04 P.g. 9731.9425 E.g. 31° 82335.81850

Name: None.

Description: Small EB IV/MB I settlement with stone circles on tributary to *Wādi al-Ġēdara*.

¶ Rothenberg, God's Wilderness, 61.

9794.05 P.g. 9716.9416 E.g. 31° 8222.8174

Name: None.

Description: Small EB IV/MB I settlement on tributary to *Wādi al-Ġēdara*.

¶ Rothenberg, God's Wilderness, 61.

9794.06 P.g. 9725.9418 E.g. 31° 8228.8175

Name: None.

Description: EB IV/MB I settlement with stone circles on edge of tributary to *Wādi al-Ġēdara* ca. 350-400m S of agricultural terraces in wādi bed.

¶ Rothenberg, God's Wilderness, 61.

9794.07 P.g. 9734.9417 E.g. 31° 8236.8178

Name: None.

Description: Very large EB IV/MB I settlement with stone circles along bank of tributary to *Wādi al-Ġēdara*. Terraced wādis ca. 200m to the SW.

¶ Rothenberg, God's Wilderness, 61.

9794.08 P.g. 9741.9419 E.g. 31° 8244.8178

Name: None.

Description: EB IV/MB I settlement with stone circles near tributary to *Wādi al-Ġēdara*.

¶ Rothenberg, God's Wilderness, 61.

9794.09 P.g. 9750.9419 E.g. 31° 8250.8177

Name: None.

Description: EB IV/MB I settlement with stone circles along tributary to *Wādi al-Ġēdara*.

¶ Rothenberg, God's Wilderness, 61.

9794.10 P.g. 9749.9416 E.g. 31° 8249.8175

Name: None.

Description: Small EB IV/MB I settlement with stone circles on tributary to *Wādi al-Ġēdara*.

¶ Rothenberg, God's Wilderness, 61.

1594.01 P.g. 1508.9448

Name: Roth 239.

Description: Scattered remains near tombs with some possibly LB/EI pottery.

¶ Courtesy of B. Rothenberg.

9493.01 P.g. 9454.9324

Name: Roth 567.

Description: Scattered remains with EB IV/MB I pottery and flints

(9493.01)

and Proto- or Early Dynastic flints.

¶ Courtesy of B. Rothenberg.

9493.02 P.g. 9433.9319

Name: Roth 565.

Description: 2 tumuli with EB IV/MB I pottery and flints and Proto- or Early Dynastic flints.

¶ Courtesy of B. Rothenberg.

1493.01 P.g. 1478.9356

Name: Roth 231.

Description: Settlement with stone circles and tombs. Pottery and flints from Chalcolithic-EB I, and possibly EB IV/MB I and LB/EI.

¶ Courtesy of B. Rothenberg.

1493.02 P.g. 1478.9328

Name: Roth 172.

Description: 2 stone enclosures (ca. 11m in diameter). Pottery and flints from Chalcolithic-EB I, and possibly EB IV/MB I and LB/EI.

¶ Courtesy of B. Rothenberg.

1493.03 P.g. 1475.9323

Name: Roth 171.

Description: Large settlement with much pottery and flints. Flints from Chalcolithic-EB I and some possibly LB/EI pottery.

¶ Courtesy of B. Rothenberg.

1493.04 P.g. 1478.9319

Name: Roth 232.

Description: Large stone circle near 2 tombs with much Chalcolithic-EB I pottery and flints.

¶ Courtesy of B. Rothenberg.

1493.05 P.g. 1480.9304

Name: Roth 170.

Description: Large settlement with many stone structures along wādi bank. Possibly pottery from Chalcolithic-EB I and EB IV/MB I.

¶ Courtesy of B. Rothenberg.

1593.01 P.g. 1536.9394

Name: Roth 31.

Description: Small EB IV/MB I site (20 x 21m) wihh stone enclosure walls between *Biqʿat Šizåfon (Wādi Abū Ǧaṯaba)* and *Biqʿat Qəṭurå (Wādi Qulēṭa)*.

¶ Rothenberg, Sfunot Negev, 138f.

1492.01 P.g. 1469.9296

Name: Roth 168.

Description: Chalcolithic-EB I settlement with many stone structures and much pottery and flints.

¶ Courtesy of B. Rothenberg.

1492.02 P.g. 1467.9295

Name: Roth 233.

Description: Chalcolithic-EB I settlement with stone circles and some possibly LB/EI pottery.

¶ Courtesy of B. Rothenberg.

1492.03 P.g. 1464.9288

Name: Roth 167 and 167A.

Description: Large settlement with circular enclosures along banks of wādi. Possibly EB IV/MB I pottery and Chalcolithic-EB I pottery and flints. Site 167A (200m from 167) also has LB/EI pottery.

¶ Courtesy of B. Rothenberg.

1492.04 P.g. 1463.9285

Name: Roth 166.

Description: Large settlement with possibly Chalcolithic-EB I pottery and flints and EB IV/MB I and LB/EI pottery.

¶ Courtesy of B. Rothenberg.

1492.05 P.g. 1467.9280

Name: Roth 234.

Description: Large Chalcolithic-EB I settlement with stone circles along banks of wādi.

¶ Courtesy of B. Rothenberg.

1492.06 P.g. 1473.9279

Name: Roth 235.

Description: Settlement along banks of wādi with a few possibly Chalcolithic-EB I flints.

¶ Courtesy of B. Rothenberg.

1492.07 P.g. 1483.9265

Name: Roth 236.

Description: Chalcolithic-EB I settlement along banks of wādi and much pottery and flints; also some possibly LB/EI pottery.

¶ Courtesy of B. Rothenberg.

1492.08 P.g. 1461.9263

Name: None.

Description: Scattered remains with possibly EB IV/MB I pottery.

¶ Courtesy of B. Rothenberg.

1592.01 P.g. 1552.9268

Name: Roth 209.

Description: Large stone structure with many Chalcolithic-EB I flints.

¶ Courtesy of B. Rothenberg.

1592.02 P.g. 1505.9257

Name: Roth 237.

Description: Cemetery with possibly Chalcolithic-EB I pottery.

¶ Courtesy of B. Rothenberg.

1592.03 P.g. 1518.9245

Name: None.

Description: LB/EI settlement on edge of *Hȧ-ʿĂrȧvȧ (Wādi al-ʿAraba)* ca. 4km NW of *ʿEn Yȯṭvȧtȧ (ʿAin ad-Dēl)*.

¶ Rothenberg, Timna, 64.

1592.04 P.g. 1553.9248

Name: Roth 213.

Description: Metallurgical site with small stone structure and tombs; possibly Chalcolithic-EB I pottery.

¶ Courtesy of B. Rothenberg.

1592.05 P.g. 1543.9233

Name: Roth 45.

Description: Large late period settlement with some possibly LB/EI pottery.

¶ Courtesy of B. Rothenberg.

1592.06 P.g. 1508.9225

Name: None.

Description: LB/EI settlement on edge of *Hȧ-ʿĂrȧvȧ (Wādi al-ʿAraba)* ca. 3 1/2km WNW of *ʿEn Yȯṭvȧtȧ (ʿAin ad-Dēl)* on one of the tributaries to *Naḥal Yoṭvȧtȧ (Wādi ad-Dēl)*.

¶ Rothenberg, Timna, 64.

1592.07 P.g. 1553.9225

Name: Roth 44.

Description: LB/EI metallurgical site on top of hill, with some possibly Chalcolithic-EB I pottery and flints.

¶ Courtesy of B. Rothenberg.

1592.08 P.g. 1561.9221

Name: Roth 205 (also 205A and 205B).

Description: Primarily Nabatean-Byzantine site, with some Chalcolithic-EB I pottery and possibly LB/EI pottery. Nearby are sites 205A and 205B where possibly LB/EI pottery was found.

¶ Courtesy of B. Rothenberg.

1592.09 P.g. 1522.9209

Name: Roth 203.

Description: 2 large stone circles with much possibly Chalcolithic-EB I pottery and flints.

¶ Courtesy of B. Rothenberg.

9591.01 P.g. 9588.9105

Name: Roth 343.

Description: Very large settlement with Chalcolithic-EB I and EB IV/MB I pottery along the *Wādi as-Sudr*, ca. 2 1/2km W of *ʿAin ed-Dēsa* and ca. 2 1/2km NNE of *ʿAin ar-Ratama*.

¶ Rothenberg, PEQ 102, 1971, 25; further, courtesy of B. Rothenberg.

9691.01 P.g. 9671.9158

Name: Roth 341.

Description: Scattered remains with Chalcolithic-EB I and EB IV/MB I pottery near several salty springs along the *Wādi as-Sudr*.

¶ Rothenberg, Museum Haaretz Bulletin 11, 1969, Pl. IV; idem, PEQ 102, 1970, 24.

1391.01 P.g. 1378.9193

Name: Roth 179.

Description: Chalcolithic-EB I settlement with stone circles and very many flints.

¶ Courtesy of B. Rothenberg.

1391.02 P.g. 1377.9168

Name: Roth 177.

Description: Chalcolithic-EB I settlement with 2 large stone enclosures and smaller attached stone circles.

¶ Courtesy of B. Rothenberg.

1391.03 P.g. 1352.9143

Name: Roth 141.

Description: Tombs with possibly Chalcolithic-EB I flints on top of hill.

¶ Courtesy of B. Rothenberg.

1391.04 P.g. 1356.9142

Name: Roth 143.

Description: Chalcolithic-EB I tombs.

¶ Courtesy of B. Rothenberg.

1391.05 P.g. 1373.9114

Name: Roth 154.

Description: Large Chalcolithic-EB I settlement with stone enclosures and tombs, and some possibly LB/EI pottery.

¶ Courtesy of B. Rothenberg.

1491.01 P.g. 1426.9193

Name: Roth 226.

Description: Settlement with large stone circles ca. 200m from spring with much Chalcolithic-EB I pottery and flints and some possibly EB IV/MB I pottery.

¶ Courtesy of B. Rothenberg.

1491.02 P.g. 1427.9160

Name: Roth 153.

Description: Small settlement with stone circles and some pottery and flints possibly dated to Chalcolithic-EB I and EB IV/MB I.

¶ Courtesy of B. Rothenberg.

1491.03 P.g. 1497.9166

Name: Roth 191.

Description: Large settlement with Chalcolithic-EB I pottery and flints (a few possibly EB IV/MB I sherds) and LB/EI pottery.

¶ Courtesy of B. Rothenberg.

1491.04 P.g. 1424.9152

Name: Roth 227.

Description: Large Chalcolithic-EB I settlement with stone circles.

¶ Courtesy of B. Rothenberg.

1491.05 P.g. 1419.9143

Name: Roth 229.

Description: Chalcolithic-EB I settlement with stone circles.

¶ Courtesy of B. Rothenberg.

1491.06 P.g. 1415.9140

Name: Roth 229A.

Description: Smelting camp in hills W of *Hȧ-ʿǍrȧvȧ (Wādi al-ʿAraba)* between *Naḥal Meteq (Wādi al-Milḥān)* and *Naḥal Berek (Wādi al-ʿUqfi)*. Pottery and flints from Chalcolithic-EB I (some possibly EB IV/MB I pottery) and LB/EI pottery.

¶ Rothenberg, Timna, 64; further, courtesy of B. Rothenberg.

1491.07 P.g. 1440.9123

Name: Roth 24.

Description: LB/EI copper mine in slopes of hills W of *Hȧ-ʿǍrȧvȧ (Wādi al-ʿAraba)* along upper reaches of *Naḥal Timnaʿ*.

¶ Rothenberg, Timna, 64. 119.

1491.08 P.g. 1447.9124

Name: Roth 25.

Description: LB/EI copper mine in slopes of hills W of *Hȧ-ʿǍrȧvȧ (Wādi al-ʿAraba)* along upper reaches of *Naḥal Timnaʿ*.

¶ Rothenberg, Timna, 64. 119.

1491.09 P.g. 1466.9129

Name: Roth 186

Description: LB/EI copper mine in slopes of hills W of *Hȧ-ʿĂrȧvȧ (Wādi al-ʿAraba)* along tributary of *Naḥal Timnaʿ*.

¶ Rothenberg, Timna, 64.

1491.10 P.g. 14245.91100

Name: None.

Description: LB/EI settlement along upper reaches of *Naḥal Timnaʿ* 200-250m W of 2 copper mines (Roth 9 + 23).

¶ Rothenberg, Timna, 64.

1491.11 P.g. 1428.9111

Name: Roth 23.

Description: LB/EI copper mine in mountains W of *Hȧ-ʿĂrȧvȧ (Wādi al-ʿAraba)* on upper reaches of *Naḥal Timnaʿ*.

¶ Rothenberg, Timna, 64.

1491.12 P.g. 1432.9117

Name: Roth 210.

Description: LB/EI copper mine in mountains W of *Hȧ-ʿĂrȧvȧ (Wādi al-ʿAraba)* on upper reaches of *Naḥal Timnaʿ*.

¶ Rothenberg, Timna, 64.

1491.13 P.g. 1431.9116

Name: Roth 211.

Description: LB/EI remains.

¶ Courtesy of B. Rothenberg.

1491.14 P.g. 1432.9115

Name: Roth 212.

Description: Copper mine in slopes of mountain W of *Hȧ-ʿĂrȧvȧ (Wādi al-ʿAraba)* along upper reaches of *Naḥal Timnaʿ*. Chalcolithic-EB I pottery and flints and LB/EI pottery.

¶ Rothenberg, Timna, 64; further, courtesy of B. Rothenberg.

1491.15 P.g. 1424.9109

Name: Roth 9.

Description: LB/EI copper mine in mountains W of *Há-ʿĂrâvá (Wādi al-ʿAraba)* on upper reaches of *Naḥal Timnaʿ*.

¶ Rothenberg, Timna, 64.

1491.16 P.g. 1426.9109

Name: Roth 18.

Description: LB/EI remains.

¶ Courtesy of B. Rothenberg.

1491.17 P.g. 1425.9107

Name: Roth 19.

Description: LB/EI remains.

¶ Courtesy of B. Rothenberg.

1491.18 P.g. 1425.9103

Name: Roth 22.

Description: Copper mine and very large smelting camp in mountains W of *Há-ʿĂrâvá (Wādi al-ʿAraba)*. Pottery from EB IV/MB I (some) and LB/EI (much).

¶ Rothenberg, PEQ 94, 1962, 11f.; idem, Timna, 64; further, courtesy of B. Rothenberg.

1491.19 P.g. 1428.9102

Name: Roth 21.

Description: Very large copper mine and smelting site. Predominantly LB/EI pottery, but some EB IV/MB I sherds.

¶ Rothenberg, PEQ 94, 1962, 11f.; further, courtesy of B. Rothenberg.

1491.20 P.g. 1448.9107

Name: Roth 2, *Ḥ. Timnaʿ*.

Description: Large (200 x 150m) excavated copper smelting camp along small tributary to *Naḥal Timnaʿ* with LB/EI pottery;

(1491.20)

LB/EI burial found.

¶ Rothenberg, Ha-Aretz 9, 1967, 53-70; idem, Timna, 64-117.

1491.21 P.g. 1456.9108

Name: Roth 15.

Description: Metallurgical site with many stone structures and LB/EI pottery on bank of *Naḥal Timnaᶜ*.

¶ Rothenberg, Timna, 64; further, courtesy of B. Rothenberg.

1491.22 P.g. 1454.9107

Name: Roth 13.

Description: Metallurgical site with 3 circles and 2 large stone enclosures and much LB/EI pottery near *Naḥal Timnaᶜ*.

¶ Rothenberg, Timna, 64f.; further, courtesy of B. Rothenberg.

1491.23 P.g. 1454.9103

Name: Roth 14.

Description: Metallurgical site with stone structures and LB/EI pottery on bank of *Naḥal Timnaᶜ*.

¶ Rothenberg, Timna, 64; further, courtesy of B. Rothenberg.

1491.24 P.g. 1451.9101

Name: Roth 3.

Description: Metallurgical site with 2 large stone enclosures and much LB/EI pottery.

¶ Rothenberg, Timna, 64f.; further, courtesy of B. Rothenberg.

1591.01 P.g. 1514.9184

Name: Roth 202.

Description: Large stone structure with Chalcolithic-EB I flints on

(1591.01)

slope of hill.

¶ Courtesy of B. Rothenberg.

1591.02 P.g. 1510.9175

Name: Roth 201.

Description: Remains with Chalcolithic-EB I and LB/EI pottery.

¶ Courtesy of B. Rothenberg.

1591.03 P.g. 1514.9161

Name: Roth 207.

Description: Scattered remains with Chalcolithic-EB I flints.

¶ Courtesy of B. Rothenberg.

1591.04 P.g. 1512.9159

Name: Roth 131.

Description: Metallurgical site with corrals ("Desert kites") and Chalcolithic-EB I flints.

¶ Courtesy of B. Rothenberg.

1591.05 P.g. 1507.9133

Name: Roth 190.

Description: Scattered remains on top of hill with Chalcolithic-EB I pottery.

¶ Courtesy of B. Rothenberg.

1591.06 P.g. 1507.9125

Name: Roth 189.

Description: Scattered remains with Chalcolithic-EB I flints on top and slopes of hill.

¶ Courtesy of B. Rothenberg.

0990.01

0990.01 P.g. 0914.9021

Name: Roth 619.

Description: Settlement with stone circles and 2 enclosures with Chalcolithic-EB I pottery and flints.

¶ Courtesy of B. Rothenberg.

0990.02 P.g. 0903.9010

Name: Roth 620.

Description: Small settlement with building remains, tumuli and enclosures with Chalcolithic-EB I flints.

¶ Courtesy of B. Rothenberg.

1090.01 P.g. 1016.9012

Name: Roth 657.

Description: Small settlement with slight stone structures and circles with Chalcolithic-EB I pottery.

¶ Courtesy of B. Rothenberg.

1390.01 P.g. 1366.9041

Name: Roth 139.

Description: Stone circle with possibly Chalcolithic-EB I flints.

¶ Courtesy of B. Rothenberg.

1390.02 P.g. 1365.9035

Name: Roth 134.

Description: Scattered remains and tombs with many possibly Chalcolithic-EB I flints.

¶ Courtesy of B. Rothenberg.

1390.03 P.g. 1377.9017

Name: Roth 133.

Description: Stone structure (13 x 10m) with possibly Chalcolithic-EB I flints.

¶ Courtesy of B. Rothenberg.

1390.04 P.g. 1380.9016

Name: Roth 132.

Description: Small settlement with a few stone circles and tombs and Chalcolithic-EB I pottery and flints.

¶ Courtesy of B. Rothenberg.

1490.01 P.g. 1447.9099

Name: Roth 12.

Description: Metallurgical site with stone buildings and LB/EI pottery on tributary to *Naḥal Timnaᶜ*.

¶ Rothenberg, Timna, 64f.; further, courtesy of B. Rothenberg.

1490.02 P.g. 1446.9093

Name: Roth 30.

Description: LB/EI copper smelting camp in *Naḥal Nəḥuštān (Wādi al-Munēᶜīya)* surrounded by large stone wall. Open cistern cut ca. 40m W of camp.

¶ Rothenberg, Timna, 64f.

1490.03 P.g. 1447.9093

Name: Roth 31.*

Description: Large EB IV/MB I settlement with stone circles and burials and some possibly Chalcolithic-EB I pottery on the top and slopes of high hill above site 1490.02.

¶ Courtesy of B. Rothenberg.

1490.04 P.g. 1457.9095

Name: Roth 195.

Description: Metallurgical site with LB/EI pottery.

¶ Courtesy of B. Rothenberg.

* Not to be confused with Roth 31, site 1593.01.

1490.05 P.g. 1457.9094

Name: Roth 194 (with Roth 196, 198, 199).

Description: Burial with LB/EI pottery ca. 20m S of 1490.04. On hilltops in immediate vicinity are 3 further findspots with LB/EI pottery, one (Roth 198) with metallurgical remains.

¶ Rothenberg, Timna, 118; further, courtesy of B. Rothenberg.

1490.06 P.g. 1450.9090

Name: Roth 34.

Description: Large copper smelting camp on top of flat hill surrounded by wall N of *Naḥal Nəḥuštān (Wādi al-Munēʿīya)*. Pottery from LB/EI.

¶ Rothenberg, Timna, 64f., 117; further, courtesy of B. Rothenberg.

1490.07 P.g. 1457.9090

Name: *Timnaʿ*, Roth 200.

Description: LB/EI temple excavated, built during reign of Sethos I, reconstructed during reign of Ramses III; also Chalcolithic-EB I pottery and flints found.

¶ Rothenberg, Timna, 64; further, courtesy of B. Rothenberg.

1490.08 P.g. 1459.9090

Name: Roth 185.

Description: LB/EI copper smelting camp with several buildings and much pottery on tributary to *Naḥal Nəḥuštān (Wādi al-Munēʿīya)*.

¶ Rothenberg, Timna, 64f.

1490.09 P.g. 1460.9092

Name: Roth 193.

Description: Small metallurgical site with LB/EI pottery.

¶ Courtesy of B. Rothenberg.

1490.10 P.g. 1497.9092

Name: Roth 188.

Description: Scattered remains on top of hill with possibly Chalcolithic-EB I pottery.

¶ Courtesy of B. Rothenberg.

1490.11 P.g. 1452.9087

Name: Roth 35.

Description: LB/EI metallurgical site with stone buildings N of *Naḥal Nəḥuštān (Wādi al-Munēʿīya)*.

¶ Rothenberg, Timna, 64; further, courtesy of B. Rothenberg.

1490.12 P.g. 1492.9084

Name: Roth 39B.

Description: Small metallurgical site with many Chalcolithic-EB I flints.

¶ Courtesy of B. Rothenberg.

1490.13 P.g. 1490.9083

Name: Roth 39.

Description: Excavated metallurgical site in *Naḥal Nəḥuštān (Wādi al-Munēʿīya)* with Chalcolithic-EB I pottery and flints and some possibly LB/EI pottery.

¶ Rothenberg, Ha-Aretz 14, 1972, 37; further, courtesy of B. Rothenberg.

1490.14 P.g. 1408.9070

Name: Roth 10.

Description: Remains with LB/EI pottery.

¶ Rothenberg, Sfunot Negev, 152f.

1490.15 P.g. 1476.9076

Name: Roth 29.

Description: Chalcolithic-EB I flints.

(1490.15)

¶ Courtesy of B. Rothenberg.

1490.16 P.g. 1492.9078

Name: Roth 39A.

Description: Metallurgical site on top of hill with Chalcolithic-EB I flints.

¶ Courtesy of B. Rothenberg.

1490.17 P.g. 1435.9068

Name: Roth 66.

Description: Copper mine with LB/EI pottery on upper reaches of *Naḥal Nəḥuštån (Wādi al-Munēʿīya).*

¶ Rothenberg, Timna, 64.

1490.18 P.g. 1478.9067

Name: Roth 42.

Description: Chalcolithic-EB I remains.

¶ Courtesy of B. Rothenberg.

1490.19 P.g. 1459.9056

Name: Roth 37.

Description: LB/EI copper mine on W bank of *Naḥal Nimrå (Wādi an-Namra).*

¶ Courtesy of B. Rothenberg.

1490.20 P.g. 1477.9031

Name: *Bəẹr ʾOrå.*

Description: EB IV/MB I settlement on top of hill overlooking *Naḥal ʾOrå* to the E.

¶ Isr. Gen. Archives: IDA.

1490.21 P.g. 1482.9036

Name: None.

Description: EB IV/MB I settlement with many circular and rectangular stone structures in *Naḥal ʾOrá*.

¶ Rothenberg, PEQ 94, 1962, 61.

1490.22 P.g. 1482.9032

Name: Roth 28.

Description: Small EB IV/MB I smelting camp on top of hill above spring near *Naḥal ʾOrá*. Stone structures with much EB IV/MB I pottery W of camp (14815.90330).

¶ Rothenberg, PEQ 94, 1962, 60; idem, Sfunot Negev, 148f.

1490.23 P.g. 1485.9008

Name: Roth 64.

Description: Small metallurgical site with possibly LB/EI pottery.

¶ Courtesy of B. Rothenberg.

1490.24 P.g. 1483.9007

Name: Roth 418.

Description: Small metallurgical site with Chalcolithic-EB I flints and LB/EI pottery.

¶ Courtesy of B. Rothenberg.

1590.01 P.g. 1528.9070

Name: Roth 26.

Description: LB/EI site in *Hà-ʿĂrává (Wādi ʿAraba)*.

¶ Rothenberg, Timna, 64; further, courtesy of B. Rothenberg.

1590.02 P.g. 1516.9039

Name: *Rogem Miqrá (Rujm Ḥadid)*, Roth 27.

Description: LB/EI site in *Hà-ʿĂrává (Wādi ʿAraba)* along *Naḥal Ráḥám*.

¶ Rothenberg, Timna, 64; further, courtesy of B. Rothenberg.

0889.01 P.g. 0882.8999

Name: Roth 337.

Description: Settlement with enclosures, round circles, and tumuli with much EB IV/MB I pottery and some Chalcolithic-EB I pottery and flints N of *Wādi Muᶜaṯiq*.

¶ Rothenberg, Ha-Aretz 11, 1969, 127; idem, PEQ 102, 1970, 24; further, courtesy of B. Rothenberg.

0889.02 P.g. 0886.8998

Name: Roth 336.

Description: Scattered remains with Chalcolithic-EB I flints and possibly Chalcolithic-EB I pottery.

¶ Rothenberg, Ha-Aretz 11, 1969, Pl.IV; further, courtesy of B. Rothenberg.

0889.03 P.g. 0894.8998

Name: Roth 621.

Description: 2 groups of stone circles and tumuli on top of hill with pottery and flints from Chalcolithic-EB I and EB IV/MB I.

¶ Courtesy of B. Rothenberg.

0889.04 P.g. 0819.8985

Name: Roth 338.

Description: Chalcolithic-EB I remains.

¶ Rothenberg, Ha-Aretz 11, 1969, Pl.IV.

0889.05 P.g. 0826.8974

Name: Roth 699.

Description: Very large EB IV/MB I settlement (ca. 1000 x 200m) with many stone enclosures (ca. 8-15m) and much pottery and flints on terrace between *Wādi aṭ-Ṭamad* and *Wādi Muᶜāṯiq*, ca. 1km S of *Bīr aṭ-Ṭamad*.

¶ Courtesy of B. Rothenberg.

1089.01 P.g. 1023.8994

Name: Roth 649

Description: Small settlement (ca. 50 x 25m) of attached stone circles with much Chalcolithic-EB I pottery and flints.

¶ Courtesy of B. Rothenberg.

1089.02 P.g. 1033.8998

Name: Roth 334.

Description: Settlement with building structures, enclosures, and tumuli. Much pottery and flints from Chalcolithic-EB I, and some possibly LB/EI pottery.

¶ Rothenberg, Ha-Aretz 11, 1969, PL.IV; further, courtesy of B. Rothenberg.

1089.03 P.g. 1044.8999

Name: Roth 333.

Description: Remains with Chalcolithic-EB I flints.

¶ Rothenberg, Ha.Aretz 11, 1969, Pl.IV; further, courtesy of B. Rothenberg.

1089.04 P.g. 1066.8997

Name: Roth 332.

Description: Remains with Chalcolithic-EB I flints.

¶ Rothenberg, Ha-Aretz 11, 1969, Pl.IV; further, courtesy of B. Rothenberg.

1089.05 P.g. 1079.8995

Name: Roth 331.

Description: Remains with Chalcolithic-EB I flints.

¶ Rothenberg, Ha-Aretz 11, 1969, Pl.IV; further, courtesy of B. Rothenberg.

1089.06 P.g. 1083.8988

Name: Roth 652.

Description: Small Chalcolithic-EB I settlement (25 x 20m) with stone

(1089.06)

buildings.

¶ Courtesy of B. Rothenberg.

1089.07 P.g. 1098.8985

Name: Roth 651.

Description: Small Chalcolithic-EB I settlement with scattered stone structures.

¶ Courtesy of B. Rothenberg.

1189.01 P.g. 1115.8999

Name: Roth 650.

Description: Chalcolithic-EB I settlement with several stone structures scattered over large area.

¶ Courtesy of B. Rothenberg.

1189.02 P.g. 1160.8991

Name: Roth 330.

Description: Remains with Chalcolithic-EB I pottery and flints.

¶ Rothenberg, Ha-Aretz 11, 1969, Pl.IV; further, courtesy of B. Rothenberg.

1189.03 P.g. 1148.8983

Name: Roth 329.

Description: Chalcolithic-EB I settlement with buildings, enclosures and tumuli, and much pottery and flints.

¶ Rothenberg, Ha-Aretz 11, 1969, 27.

1189.04 P.g. 1157.8982

Name: Roth 328.

Description: Remains with Chalcolithic-EB I flints on protected slope of hill.

¶ Rothenberg, Ha-Aretz 11, 1969, 27; further, courtesy of B. Rothenberg.

1389.01 P.g. 1368.8992

Name: Roth 144.

Description: Large Chalcolithic-EB I settlement with scattered stone structures and tombs and much pottery and flints.

¶ Courtesy of B. Rothenberg.

1389.02 P.g. 1377.8997

Name: Roth 146A.

Description: Scattered remains with 2 tombs and much pottery and some possibly Chalcolithic-EB I flints.

¶ Courtesy of B. Rothenberg.

1389.03 P.g. 1376.8994.

Name: Roth 146.

Description: Remains with many Chalcolithic-EB I flints.

¶ Courtesy of B. Rothenberg.

1389.04 P.g. 1389.8971

Name: Roth 225.

Description: Scattered remains on hill with possibly Chalcolithic-EB I pottery and flints.

¶ Courtesy of B. Rothenberg.

1389.05 P.g. 1325.8912

Name: Roth 618.

Description: Settlement with round stone circles, enclosures, and tumuli, with Chalcolithic-EB I pottery and flints and possibly EB IV/MB I pottery.

¶ Courtesy of B. Rothenberg.

1489.01 P.g. 1432.8959

Name: None.

Description: Scattered remains on slope of hill near *Naḥal ᶜAmràm*. Pottery from MB II and possibly from EB IV/MB I and LB.

¶ Survey of Israel: IDA.

1489.02 P.g. 1439.8958

Name: Roth 32.

Description: Remains with LB/EI pottery on N bank of *Naḥal ᶜAmrâm*.

¶ Courtesy of B. Rothenberg.

1489.03 P.g. 1438.8956

Name: Roth 33.

Description: LB/EI metallurgical site with much scattered pottery and stones on slope of hill near *Naḥal ᶜAmrân*.

¶ Rothenberg, Timna, 64; further, courtesy of B. Rothenberg.

1489.04. P.g. 1437.8948

Name: Roth 33A.

Description: LB/EI copper mine and smelting camp on *Har ʾĂmir* between *Naḥal ᶜAmrâm* and *Naḥal Šəḥoret*.

¶ Rothenberg, Timna, 64; further, courtesy of B. Rothenberg.

1489.05 P.g. 1430.8921

Name: Roth 119.

Description: Scattered remains over large area with possibly EB IV/MB I pottery.

¶ Courtesy of B. Rothenberg.

1489.06 P.g. 1445.8919

Name: Roth 81.

Description: Tombs and 2 large stone circles with Chalcolithic-EB I flints.

¶ Courtesy of B. Rothenberg.

1489.07 P.g. 1424.8809

Name: Roth 122.

Description: Remains with possibly Chalcolithic-EB I flints.

¶ Courtesy of B. Rothenberg.

9788.01 P.g. 9741.8897

Name: Roth 691.

Description: Settlement with 3 small groups of enclosures with much Egyptian Proto-dynastic pottery and flints and some Old Kingdom pottery.

¶ Courtesy of B. Rothenberg.

9788.02 P.g. 9753.8894

Name: Roth 689.

Description: Small settlement with 3 oval enclosures with secondarily attached tumuli with Egyptian Proto-dynastic pottery and flints on E bank of *Wādi Umm Ǧidla*.

¶ Courtesy of B. Rothenberg.

9788.03 P.g. 9750.8872

Name: Roth 688.

Description: Settlement (ca. 100 x 75m) with Nawami-type structures, metallurgical remains and much Egyptian Proto-dynastic pottery and flints. Burials with possibly EB IV/MB I pottery.

¶ Courtesy of B. Rothenberg.

9788.04 P.g. 9772.8879

Name: Roth 687.

Description: Circle (20m diameter) of low tumuli with possibly Egyptian Proto- or early- dynastic pottery. Site lies on open plain.

¶ Courtesy of B. Rothenberg.

9888.01 P.g. 9816.8800

Name: Roth 679.

Description: Small settlement on high plateau with large circular enclosure and nearby smaller enclosure. Possibly Chalcolithic-EB I or EB IV/MB I pottery and flints.

¶ Courtesy of B. Rothenberg.

0588.01 P.g. 0589.8857

Name: Roth 629.

Description: Enclosures and tumuli with Chalcolithic-EB I pottery and flints and some possibly EB pottery.

¶ Courtesy of B. Rothenberg.

0788.01 P.g. 0770.8817

Name: Roth 624.

Description: Settlement with 2 enclosures and small stone circle with Chalcolithic-EB I flints.

¶ Courtesy of B. Rothenberg.

0788.02 P.g. 0773.8815

Name: Roth 625.

Description: Chalcolithic-EB I settlement with 3 groups of building remains and much pottery and flints.

¶ Courtesy of B. Rothenberg.

1288.01 P.g. 1252.8873

Name: Roth 324.

Description: Copper mine with adjacent smelting camp; possibly LB/EI.

¶ Rothenberg, Ha-Aretz 11, 1969, 24.

1288.02 P.g. 1258.8873

Name: Roth 323.

Description: Remains with Chalcolithic-EB I pottery and flints.

¶ Rothenberg, Ha-Aretz 11, 1969, Pl.IV; further, courtesy of B. Rothenberg.

1288.03 P.g. 1299.8879

Name: Roth 322.

Description: Remains with Chalcolithic-EB I flints.

¶ Rothenberg, Ha-Aretz 11, 1969, Pl.IV; further, courtesy of B. Rothenberg.

1388.01 P.g. 1315.8887

Name: Roth 320.

Description: Remains with Chalcolithic-EB I flints.

¶ Rothenberg, Ha-Aretz 11, 1969, Pl.IV; further, courtesy of B. Rothenberg.

1388.02 P.g. 1317.8882

Name: Roth 584.

Description: Small settlement (ca. 10 x 10m) with circular stone building and Chalcolithic-EB I pottery and flints.

¶ Courtesy of B. Rothenberg.

1388.03 P.g. 1317.8877

Name: Roth 310.

Description: Remains with Chalcolithic-EB I flints.

¶ Ronen, PEQ 1970, 30-41; Rothenberg, Ha-Aretz 11, 1969, Pl.IV; further, courtesy of B. Rothenberg.

1388.04 P.g. 1319.8874

Name: Roth 321.

Description: Remains with Chalcolithic-EB I flints.

¶ Courtesy of B. Rothenberg.

1388.05 P.g. 1324.8876

Name: Roth 311.

Description: Remains with Chalcolithic-EB I pottery and flints.

¶ Rothenberg, Ha-Aretz 11, 1969, 24.Pl.IV; further, courtesy of B. Rothenberg.

1388.06 P.g. 1323.8873

Name: Roth 312.

Description: Chalcolithic-EB I remains.

¶ Rothenberg, Ha-Aretz 11, 1969, Pl.IV.

1388.07 P.g. 1391.8871

Name: Roth 86.

Description: Tombs with a little LB/EI pottery in hills WNW of *ʾẸlat* on upper reaches of *Naḥal Šəlomo*.

¶ Rothenberg, Timna, 64; further, courtesy of B. Rothenberg.

1388.08 P.g. 1392.8836

Name: Roth 217.

Description: LB/EI copper mine on *Har Rəḥabʿâm* near *Naḥal Rəḥabʿâm*.

¶ Rothenberg, Timna, 64.

1488.01 P.g. 1425.8882

Name: Roth 82.

Description: Scattered remains with LB/EI pottery over large area along banks of wādi.

¶ Courtesy of B. Rothenberg.

1488.02 P.g. 1462.8879

Name: Roth 46.

Description: Metallurgical site with possibly Chalcolithic-EB I and LB/EI pottery.

¶ Courtesy of B. Rothenberg.

1488.03 P.g. 1448.8842

Name: Roth 40.

Description: Metallurgical site with 2 stone enclosures with some possibly EB IV/MB I pottery on top of hill above *ʾẸlat*.

¶ Isr. Gen. Archives: IDA; Rothenberg, PEQ 94, 1962, 61; further, courtesy of B. Rothenberg.

1488.04 P.g. 1476.8845

Name: *Tall al-Ḫulēfa*.

Description: Excavated LB/EI copper smelting camp in *Wādi ʿAraba (Hå-ʿĂråvå)* at head of the *Gulf of ʿAqaba (Gulf of ʾẸlat)*.

(1488.04)

¶ Rothenberg, Timna, 64.

1488.05 P.g. 1400.8823

Name: Roth 215.

Description: Large stone structure with Chalcolithic-EB I pottery and flints.

¶ Courtesy of B. Rothenberg.

9787.01 P.g. 9766.8786

Name: Roth 684.

Description: EB settlement with many enclosures and much pottery and flints on flat terrace above and ca. 200m W of spring.

¶ Courtesy of B. Rothenberg.

9887.01 P.g. 9837.8789

Name: Roth 677.

Description: EB IV/MB I settlement with several large enclosures on flat plateau at junction of *Wādi al-Bayāḍ* and *Wādi aš-Šallāla*.

¶ Courtesy of B. Rothenberg.

9887.02 P.g. 9834.8786

Name: Roth 678.

Description: Tomb on high ridge with possibly Egyptian Proto-dynastic flints.

¶ Courtesy of B. Rothenberg.

9887.03 P.g. 9863.8771

Name: Roth 692.

Description: Large settlement with much EB IV/MB I pottery and flints and many mainly circular enclosures above wide wādi; several EB IV/MB I burials nearby.

¶ Courtesy of B. Rothenberg.

9887.04 P.g. 9857.8765

Name: Roth 676.

Description: Large burial ground (ca. 1000 x 200m) on top of high ridge at juncture of *Wādi Qisil* and *Wādi Ṭurēfa*. Pottery: Egyptian Proto-dynastic, Chalcolithic-EB I, EB, and possibly EB IV/MB I.

¶ Courtesy of B. Rothenberg.

9887.05 P.g. 9856.8765

Name: Roth 552.

Description: Settlement on W slope of 9887.04 with some stone circles and many tumuli with much EB IV/MB I pottery and flints and some Egyptian possibly Proto- or early dynastic flints.

¶ Courtesy of B. Rothenberg.

9987.01 P.g. 9915.8704

Name: Roth 547.

Description: EB IV/MB I settlement with 2 large enclosures and 2 small attached structures.

¶ Courtesy of B. Rothenberg.

0587.01 P.g. 0579.8759

Name: Roth 630.

Description: Building (ca. 3m diameter) and 5 tumuli with Chalcolithic-EB I flints.

¶ Courtesy of B. Rothenberg.

1387.01 P.g. 1362.8748

Name: *Ǧazīrat Firʿaun*, Roth 43.

Description: Island, ca. 3-400m off coast of Sinai with some metallurgical remains and LB/EI pottery and 3 possibly EB IV/MB I sherds.

¶ Rothenberg, Ha-Aretz 11, 1969, Pl.IV; idem, Timna, 202-07; further, courtesy of B. Rothenberg.

1387.02 P.g. 1315.8701

Name: Roth 413.

Description: Large stone circle (ca. 8-10m diameter), with some possibly Chalcolithic-EB I or EB flints.

¶ Courtesy of B. Rothenberg.

9786.01 P.g. 9732.8624

Name: Roth 537.

Description: Large settlement (ca. 100 x 100m) with enclosures and tumuli, with Chalcolithic-EB I pottery and flints and possibly EB IV/MB I pottery.

¶ Courtesy of B. Rothenberg.

9886.01 P.g. 9838.8682

Name: Roth 550.

Description: Settlement with EB IV/MB I pottery, possibly Egyptian Proto- or early dynastic flints and some possibly Chalcolithic-EB I pottery.

¶ Courtesy of B. Rothenberg.

9886.02 P.g. 9843.8665

Name: Roth 549.

Description: Very large Chalcolithic-EB I cemetery (over ca. 1500m area) on top of plateau.

¶ Courtesy of B. Rothenberg.

9886.03 P.g. 9802.8636

Name: Roth 540.

Description: Remains with EB IV/MB I pottery.

¶ Courtesy of B. Rothenberg.

9986.01 P.g. 9944.8697

Name: Roth 546.

Description: Small EB IV/MB I settlement (ca. 50 x 20m) with attached

(9986.01)

stone structures and much pottery and flints.

¶ Courtesy of B. Rothenberg.

9986.02 P.g. 9944.8695

Name: Roth 545.

Description: EB IV/MB I settlement with stone enclosure and much pottery and flints.

¶ Courtesy of B. Rothenberg.

0086.01 P.g. 0014.8631

Name: Roth 695.

Description: Large settlement with round structures above *ᶜAin Yarqa*, with some Egyptian, possibly Proto- dynastic pottery and flints.

¶ Courtesy of B. Rothenberg.

0586.01 P.g. 0548.8685

Name: Roth 631.

Description: Circular structures and wall ca. 17-21m long with Chalcolithic-EB I flints.

¶ Courtesy of B. Rothenberg.

0586.02 P.g. 0570.8678

Name: Roth 632.

Description: Small settlement with stone structures and a few tumuli with Chalcolithic-EB I flints.

¶ Courtesy of B. Rothenberg.

0586.03 P.g. 0578.8663

Name: Roth 634.

Description: Stone circles: flint workshop with some possible tombs. Flints from Chalcolithic-EB I.

¶ Courtesy of B. Rothenberg.

0586.04 P.g. 0596.8605

Name: Roth 635.

Description: Chalcolithic-EB I settlement with large enclosure and stone circles and much pottery and flints.

¶ Courtesy of B. Rothenberg.

1086.01 P.g. 1074.8663

Name: Roth 393.

Description: Chalcolithic-EB I remains.

¶ Rothenberg, Ha-Aretz 11, 1969, Pl.IV.

1386.01 P.g. 1394.8673

Name: Roth 414.

Description: Settlement with many stone circles and small tumuli built against side of hill with EB flints and some possibly Chalcolithic-EB I pottery.

¶ Courtesy of B. Rothenberg.

0085.01 P.g. 003.852 E.g. 31° 8589.7288

Name: *ʿAin Abū al-Nutēqina*, Roth 696.

Description: Oasis with numerous enclosures and square and round houses with Egyptian Proto-dynastic pottery.

¶ Courtesy of B. Rothenberg.

0085.02 P.g. 003.852 E.g. 31° 8590.7289

Name: Roth 697.

Description: Settlement with several houses and much pottery and flints, some from EB and some Egyptian possibly Proto-dynastic pottery.

¶ Courtesy of B. Rothenberg.

0685.01 P.g. 0649.8550

Name: Roth 636.

Description: Tumuli with many Chalcolithic-EB I flints.

¶ Courtesy of B. Rothenberg.

0685.02 P.g. 0651.8545

Name: Roth 637.

Description: Settlement with circles and attached enclosures with many Chalcolithic-EB I flints.

¶ Courtesy of B. Rothenberg.

0685.03 P.g. 0653.8516

Name: Roth 638.

Description: Burial site with different types of tumuli with Chalcolithic-EB I flints.

¶ Courtesy of B. Rothenberg.

0685.04 P.g. 0648.8504

Name: Roth 639.

Description: Small settlement with enclosure, 2 circles and tumuli with Chalcolithic-EB I flints.

¶ Courtesy of B. Rothenberg.

0084.01 P.g. 000.842 E.g. 31° 8555.7189

Name: Roth 535.

Description: Chalcolithic-EB I cairn burials and tumuli.

¶ Courtesy of B. Rothenberg.

0684.01 P.g. 0628.8464

Name: Roth 640.

Description: Chalcolithic-EB I settlement with Nawami-like structures and enclosures and tumuli nearby.

¶ Courtesy of B. Rothenberg.

9883.01 P.g. 988.830 E.g. 31° 8435.7074

Name: Roth 349A.

Description: Metallurgical site with Egyptian inscription from Proto-dynastic period.

¶ Courtesy of B. Rothenberg.

9883.02 P.g. 988.830 E.g. 31° 8436.7068

Name: Roth 349.

Description: Turquoise mine with 5th (Sahuré) and 12th (Sesostris I) dynasty cartouches!

¶ Courtesy of B. Rothenberg.

9983.01 P.g. 998.835 E.g. 31° 8540.7125

Name: Roth 354.

Description: Remains with possibly LB/EI pottery.

¶ Rothenberg, Ha-Aretz 11, 1969, Pl.IV.

9983.02 P.g. 991.832 E.g. 31° 8469.7088

Name: Roth 344A.

Description: New Kingdom inscription.

¶ Courtesy of B. Rothenberg.

9983.03 P.g. 991.832 E.g. 31° 8470.7089

Name: Roth 344.

Description: Metallurgical site with Egyptian Proto-dynastic, LB/EI, and possibly EB IV/MB I pottery.

¶ Rothenberg, Ha-Aretz 11, 1969, Pl.IV; further, courtesy of B. Rothenberg.

0683.01 P.g. 0641.8377

Name: Roth 647.

Description: Large settlement with tumuli and much Chalcolithic-EB I pottery and flints.

¶ Courtesy of B. Rothenberg.

0683.02 P.g. 0647.8373

Name: Roth 646.

Description: Scattered Chalcolithic-EB I remains with tumuli.

¶ Courtesy of B. Rothenberg.

0683.03 P.g. 0649.8371

Name: Roth 645.

Description: Small enclosure with Chalcolithic-EB I flints.

¶ Courtesy of B. Rothenberg.

0683.04 P.g. 0652.8368

Name: Roth 644.

Description: Large circle (ca. 33m diameter) with attached structures; Chalcolithic-EB I pottery and flints.

¶ Courtesy of B. Rothenberg.

0683.05 P.g. 0658.8366

Name: Roth 642.

Description: Large settlements and burials with Chalcolithic-EB I flints.

¶ Courtesy of B. Rothenberg.

0683.06 P.g. 0654.8362

Name: Roth 643.

Description: Very large burial site with Chalcolithic-EB I flints.

¶ Courtesy of B. Rothenberg.

0683.07 P.g. 0618.8320

Name: Roth 516.

Description: Settlement with scattered structures over large area with Chalcolithic-EB I flints.

¶ Courtesy of B. Rothenberg.

0683.08 P.g. 0617.8318

Name: Roth 515.

Description: Very large settlement with many enclosures over large area with Chalcolithic-EB I flints.

¶ Courtesy of B. Rothenberg.

0683.09 P.g. 0627.8308

Name: Roth 514.

Description: Chalcolithic-EB I settlement with 2 enclosures and tumulus.

¶ Courtesy of B. Rothenberg.

0983.01 P.g. 0942.8304

Name: *ʿAin al-Aḥmad*, Roth 510.

Description: Settlement with enclosures and tumuli on terrace above spring with EB pottery and flints and possibly Chalcolithic-EB I pottery.

¶ Courtesy of B. Rothenberg.

1083.01 P.g. 1055.8330

Name: Roth 399.

Description: Remains with possibly Chalcolithic-EB I pottery.

¶ Rothenberg, Ha-Aretz, 11, 1969, Pl.IV; further, courtesy of B. Rothenberg.

9882.01 P.g. 981.820 E.g. 31° 8369.6967

Name: Roth 348.

Description: Remains with Chalcolithic-EB I flints.

¶ Rothenberg, Ha-Aretz 11, 1969, Pl.IV; further, courtesy of B. Rothenberg.

9982.01 P.g. 9939.8298 E.g. 31° 8492.7066

Name: Roth 352.

Description: Copper mine in hills E of *Bīr Naṣb* with pottery from MB II and LB.

¶ Rothenberg, PEQ 102, 1970, 25.

9982.02 P.g. 9935.8292 E.g. 31° 8488.7060

Name: *Bīr naṣb*, Roth 350.

Description: Large metallurgical site with several buildings and much Egyptian Proto-dynastic, MB II, and LB pottery.

¶ Petrie, Researches in Sinai, 1906, 27; Rothenberg, Ha-Aretz 11, 1969, 31; idem, PEQ 102, 1970, 25; further, courtesy of B. Rothenberg.

9982.03 P.g. 9938.8292 E.g. 31° 8491.7060

Name: Roth 351.

Description: On path to copper mine (9982.01), 3 Proto-Sinaitic inscriptions and 1 Egyptian stela (18th.-15th. cent.).

¶ Rothenberg, Ha-Aretz 11, 1969, 31f; idem, PEQ 102, 1970, 25; further, courtesy of B. Rothenberg.

9982.04 P.g. 999.829 E.g. 31° 8544.7058

Name: *Sarābīt al-Ḫādim*, Roth 355.

Description: Excavated Egyptian temple from Middle and New Kingdom; nearby EB IV/MB I stone circles reported; also Egyptian Proto-dynastic pottery and EB flints reported.

¶ Rothenberg, God's Wilderness, 182; idem, Ha-Aretz 11, 1969, Pl.IV; Isr. Gen. Archives: IDA; further, courtesy of B. Rothenberg.

0082.01 P.g. 008.822 E.g. 31° 8640.6997

Name: Roth 533.

Description: Small EB settlement with enclosures and burial tumuli.

¶ Courtesy of B. Rothenberg.

0182.01 P.g. 010.820 E.g. 31° 8660.6970

Name: Roth 531.

Description: Settlement with several small enclosures and flints that are possibly Chalcolithic-EB I or EB.

¶ Courtesy of B. Rothenberg.

0682.01 P.g. 0626.8297

Name: Roth 513.

Description: 1 stone circle with Chalcolithic-EB I flints ca. 200m from *Bīr al-Biyār*.

¶ Courtesy of B. Rothenberg.

0682.02 P.g. 0666.8275

Name: Roth 517.

Description: Large circle (23 x 26m) with 2 attached rooms, with Chalcolithic-EB I flints.

¶ Courtesy of B. Rothenberg.

0682.03 P.g. 0685.8261

Name: Roth 518.

Description: Very large settlement (ca. 500 x 150m) with many enclosures, with Chalcolithic-EB I flints.

¶ Courtesy of B. Rothenberg.

0782.01 P.g. 0757.8278

Name: Roth 520.

Description: 2 enclosures (ca. 11 x 9m) with Chalcolithic-EB I flints.

¶ Courtesy of B. Rothenberg.

0782.02 P.g. 0749.8267

Name: Roth 519.

Description: Very large settlement with several groups of enclosures, with Chalcolithic-EB I flints.

¶ Courtesy of B. Rothenberg.

0782.03 P.g. 0746.8219

Name: Roth 507.

Description: Large Chalcolithic-EB I settlement (ca. 170 x 90m) with Nawami-like stone structures.

¶ Courtesy of B. Rothenberg.

0882.01 P.g. 0878.8247

Name: Roth 509A.

Description: Very large cemetery with many tumuli along ridge of hill, with Chalcolithic-EB I flints.

¶ Courtesy of B. Rothenberg.

0982.01 P.g. 0904.8260

Name: Roth 511.

Description: 7 Nawami-like structures with Chalcolithic-EB I flints.

¶ Courtesy of B. Rothenberg.

0982.02 P.g. 0900.8258

Name: Roth 511A.

Description: 6-7 Nawami-like structures wtth Chalcolithic-EB I flints.

¶ Courtesy of B. Rothenberg.

1082.01 P.g. 1061.8295

Name: Roth 398.

Description: Remains with Chalcolithic-EB I flints.

¶ Rothenberg, Ha-Aretz 11, 1969, Pl.IV; further, courtesy of B. Rothenberg.

9881.01 P.g. 988.810 E.g. 31° 8434.6868

Name: Roth 359.

Description: Remains with Chalcolithic-EB I flints.

¶ Rothenberg, Ha-Aretz 11, 1969, Pl.IV; further, courtesy of B. Rothenberg.

9981.01 P.g. 991.815 E.g. 31° 847.691

Name: Roth 357.

Description: Middle Kingdom turquoise mines.

¶ Courtesy of B. Rothenberg.

0181.01 P.g. 018.810 E.g. 31° 8732.6874

Name: Roth 527.

Description: 2 enclosures and tumulus on slope of hill with Chalcolithic-EB I pottery and flints.

¶ Courtesy of B. Rothenberg.

0681.01 P.g. 0623.8164

Name: Roth 521.

Description: Several large enclosures and stone circles on slope of hill with Chalcolithic-EB I flints.

¶ Courtesy of B. Rothenberg.

0681.02 P.g. 0676.8165

Name: Roth 506.

Description: Very large settlement with several groups of attached enclosures and tumuli with Chalcolithic-EB I flints.

¶ Courtesy of B. Rothenberg.

0681.03 P.g. 0609.8148.

Name: Roth 502.

Description: Stone structures and tumuli on terrace of wādi with Chalcolithic-EB I flints.

¶ Courtesy of B. Rothenberg.

0681.04 P.g. 0647.8145

Name: Roth 505.

Description: Settlement with 2 houses, enclosures and tumuli, with Chalcolithic-EB I flints.

¶ Courtesy of B. Rothenberg.

0681.05 P.g. 0617.8124

Name: Roth 504.

Description: Very large settlement on alluvial terrace with stone structures and many Chalcolithic-EB I flints.

¶ Courtesy of B. Rothenberg.

0681.06 P.g. 0632.8127

Name: Roth 503A-G.

Description: Very large settlement over ca. 2000m area with Nawami-like structures and possibly Chalcolithic-EB I pottery.

¶ Courtesy of B. Rothenberg.

0981.01 P.g. 0935.8125

Name: Roth 397.

Description: Remains with possibly Chalcolithic-EB I or EB flints.

¶ Rothenberg, Ha-Aretz 11, 1969, Pl.IV; further, courtesy of B. Rothenberg.

9980.01 P.g. 993.809 E.g. 31° 8485.6861

Name: Roth 360.

Description: Remains with Chalcolithic-EB I flints.

¶ Rothenberg, Ha-Aretz 11, 1969, Pl.IV; further, courtesy of B. Rothenberg.

9980.02 P.g. 996.800 E.g. 31° 8513.7868

Name: Roth 372.

Description: Remains with Chalcolithic-EB I flints.

¶ Rothenberg, Ha-Aretz 11, 1969, Pl.IV; further, courtesy of B. Rothenberg.

0080.01 P.g. 001.803 E.g. 31° 8566.6797

Name: Roth 363.

Description: Chalcolithic-EB I remains.

(0080.01)

¶ Rothenberg, Ha-Aretz 11, 1969, Pl.IV.

0080.02 P.g. 003.801 E.g. 31° 8587.6784

Name: Roth 369.

Description: Remains with Chalcolithic-EB I flints.

¶ Rothenberg, Ha-Aretz 11, 1969, Pl.IV; further, courtesy of B. Rothenberg.

0480.01 P.g. 043.805 E.g. 31° 9001.6836

Name: Roth 465.

Description: Large Chalcolithic-EB I settlement with Nawami-like structures, several large enclosures and 1 tumulus.

¶ Courtesy of B. Rothenberg.

0480.02 P.g. 046.804 E.g. 31° 9031.6831

Name: Roth 461.

Description: Group of attached structures over area ca. 45 x 20m, with Chalcolithic-EB I flints.

¶ Courtesy of B. Rothenberg.

0480.03 P.g. 048.800 E.g. 31° 9044.6786

Name: Roth 462.

Description: Chalcolithic-EB I settlement with Nawami-like structures, enclosures and small circles.

¶ Courtesy of B. Rothenberg.

0580.01 P.g. 0529.8092

Name: Roth 522A.

Description: Scattered remains over small area (20 x 20m) with much possibly Chalcolithic-EB I or EB pottery and flints.

¶ Courtesy of B. Rothenberg.

0780.01 P.g. 0772.8015

Name: Roth 495.

Description: Large group of stone structures with some tombs, with possibly Chalcolithic-EB I or EB flints.

¶ Courtesy of B. Rothenberg.

0780.02 P.g. 0771.8012

Name: Roth 494.

Description: Very large settlement with enclosures, stone circles and tumuli with possibly Chalcolithic-EB I or EB flints.

¶ Courtesy of B. Rothenberg.

0780.03 P.g. 0784.8000

Name: Roth 491.

Description: 2 stone structures in area 50 x 25m with possibly Chalcolithic-EB I or EB pottery and flints.

¶ Courtesy of B. Rothenberg.

0880.01 P.g. 0878.8076

Name: Roth 388.

Description: Chalcolithic-EB I remains.

¶ Rothenberg, Ha-Aretz 11, 1969, Pl.IV.

0880.02 P.g. 0874.8006

Name: Roth 389.

Description: Chalcolithic-EB I remains.

¶ Rothenberg, Ha-Aretz 11, 1969, Pl.IV.

9879.01 P.g. 989.798 E.g. 31° 8449.6751

Name: Roth 371.

Description: Remains with Chalcolithic-EB I flints.

¶ Rothenberg, Ha-Aretz 11, 1969, Pl.IV; further, courtesy of B. Rothenberg.

9879.02 P.g. 983.791 E.g. 31° 8392.6682

Name: Roth 370.

Description: Remains with Chalcolithic-EB I flints.

¶ Rothenberg, Ha-Aretz 11, 1969, Pl.IV; further, courtesy of B. Rothenberg.

9979.01 P.g. 997.792 E.g. 31° 8526.6689

Name: Roth 364.

Description: Remains with Egyptian Proto-dynastic and LB/EI pottery.

¶ Rothenberg, Ha-Aretz 11, 1969, Pl.IV; further, courtesy of B. Rothenberg.

0179.01 P.g. 010.794 E.g. 31° 8659.6714

Name: Roth 368.

Description: Remains with Chalcolithic-EB I pottery and flints.

¶ Rothenberg, Ha-Aretz 11, 1969, Pl.IV; further, courtesy of B. Rothenberg.

0179.02 P.g. 012.794 E.g. 31° 8676.6708

Name: Roth 366.

Description: Remains with Chalcolithic-EB I pottery and flints.

¶ Courtesy of B. Rothenberg.

0179.03 P.g. 011.793 E.g. 31° 8664.6703

Name: Roth 367.

Description: Remains with Chalcolithic-EB I pottery and flints, and LB/EI pottery.

¶ Rothenberg, Ha-Aretz 11, 1969, Pl.IV; further, courtesy of B. Rothenberg.

0179.04 P.g. 017.791 E.g. 31° 8730.6683

Name: Roth 373.

Description: Remains with Chalcolithic-EB I pottery and flints, and some possibly LB/EI pottery.

¶ Courtesy of B. Rothenberg.

0279.01 P.g. 020.792 E.g. 31° 8759.6692

Name: Roth 374.

Description: Remains with possibly Chalcolithic-EB I or EB pottery and flints.

¶ Rothenberg, Ha-Aretz 11, 1969, Pl.IV; further, courtesy of B. Rothenberg.

0279.02 P.g. 0237.7910 E.g. 31° 8790.6678

Name: Roth 375.

Description: Settlement with houses and tumuli on N bank of *wādi aš-šēḫ*, with possibly Chalcolithic-EB I or EB pottery and flints.

¶ Rothenberg, Ha-Aretz 11, 1969, Pl.IV; idem, PEQ 102, 1970, 27; further, courtesy of B. Rothenberg.

0379.01 P.g. 037.799 E.g. 31° 8937.6775

Name: Roth 468.

Description: 2 large enclosures with several tumuli with possibly Chalcolithic-EB I or EB pottery and flints.

¶ Courtesy of B. Rothenberg.

0379.02 P.g. 039.799 E.g. 31° 8957.6777

Name: Roth 469.

Description: Group of attached enclosures (ca. 25 x 20m) with possibly Chalcolithic-EB I or EB pottery and flints.

¶ Courtesy of B. Rothenberg.

0479.01 P.g. 041.798 E.g. 31° 8977.6766

Name: Roth 471.

Description: Tumuli with possibly Chalcolithic-EB I or EB flints.

¶ Courtesy of B. Rothenberg.

0479.02 P.g. 049.798 E.g. 31° 9058.6768

Name: Roth 460.

Description: Settlement with group of stone structures with possibly

(0479.02)

Chalcolithic-EB I or EB pottery and flints.

¶ Courtesy of B. Rothenberg.

0479.03 P.g. 042.790 E.g. 31° 8991.6691

Name: Roth 378.

Description: Remains with EB flints.

¶ Rothenberg, Ha-Aretz 11, 1969, Pl.IV; further, courtesy of B. Rothenberg.

0479.04 P.g. 044.790 E.g. 31° 9006.6687

Name: Roth 379.

Description: Settlement with Nawami-like structures with Chalcolithic-EB I pottery and flints.

¶ Rothenberg, Ha-Aretz 11, 1969, Pl.IV; further, courtesy of B. Rothenberg.

0479.05 P.g. 0492.7909

Name: Ophir 1042.

Description: Excavated EB settlement (150 x 80m) on *wādi aš-Šēḫ*.

¶ Courtesy of I. Beit-Arieh.

0579.01 P.g. 0507.7993

Name: Roth 501.

Description: Settlement (120 x 60m) with Nawami-like structures and stone circles with possibly Chalcolithic-EB I pottery and flints.

¶ Courtesy of B. Rothenberg.

0579.02 P.g. 0580.7926

Name: Roth 473.

Description: Scattered remains with possibly Chalcolithic-EB I or EB pottery and flints.

¶ Courtesy of B. Rothenberg.

0579.03 P.g. 0586.7927

Name: Roth 474.

Description: Very large settlement with Nawami-like structures, stone circles, and tumuli with possibly Chalcolithic-EB I or EB pottery and flints.

¶ Courtesy of B. Rothenberg.

0579.04 P.g. 0557.7914

Name: Roth 472.

Description: 2 large stone circles on slope of hill with Chalcolithic-EB I pottery and flints.

¶ Courtesy of B. Rothenberg.

0579.05 P.g. 0519.7919

Name: Ophir 1016.

Description: EB remains near wādi.

¶ Courtesy of I. Beit-Arieh.

0579.06 P.g. 0515.7915

Name: Ophir 1017.

Description: Small EB settlement near wādi.

¶ Courtesy of I. Beit-Arieh.

0579.07 P.g. 0523.7912

Name: Ophir 1024.

Description: Remains with possibly EB pottery.

¶ Courtesy of I. Beit-Arieh.

0579.08 P.g. 0534.7918

Name: Ophir 1023.

Description: EB settlement (35 x 20m) with 6-7 rooms and stone circles.

¶ Courtesy of I. Beit-Arieh.

0579.09 P.g. 0532.7916

Name: Ophir 1022.

Description: EB settlement (30 x 30m) with 10 rooms and stone circles.

¶ Courtesy of I. Beit-Arieh.

0579.10 P.g. 0531.7915

Name: Ophir 1020.

Description: 4 tumuli with possibly EB pottery.

¶ Courtesy of I. Beit-Arieh.

0579.11 P.g. 0530.7914

Name: Ophir 1021.

Description: Settlement (ca. 50 x 50m) with 12 rooms and stone circles, with possibly EB pottery.

¶ Courtesy of I. Beit-Arieh.

0579.12 P.g. 0502.7902

Name: Ophir 1014.

Description: Settlement (25 x 30m) with EB pottery.

¶ Courtesy of I. Beit-Arieh.

0779.01 P.g. 0756.7997

Name: Roth 496.

Description: Stone structure (21 x 15m) and tumuli with possibly Chalcolithic-EB I or EB flints.

¶ Courtesy of B. Rothenberg.

0779.02 P.g. 0774.7973

Name: Roth 391.

Description: Remains with possibly Chalcolithic-EB I or EB flints.

¶ Courtesy of B. Rothenberg.

0779.03 P.g. 0743.7958

Name: Roth 499.

Description: Settlement (ca. 80 x 120m) with stone circles on terrace above wādi with some possibly Chalcolithic-EB I or EB pottery and flints.

¶ Courtesy of B. Rothenberg.

0879.01 P.g. 0838.7997

Name: Roth 392.

Description: Remains with possibly Chalcolithic-EB I or EB flints.

¶ Rothenberg, Ha-Aretz 11, 1969, Pl.IV; further, courtesy of B. Rothenberg.

0478.01 P.g. 0492.7899

Name: Ophir 1044.

Description: EB settlement (ca. 100 x 30m) with 10 stone circles and 4 rooms on *Wādi aš-Šēḫ*.

¶ Courtesy of I. Beit-Arieh.

0478.02 P.g. 0493.7884

Name: *Šēḫ Muḥsin*.

Description: Very large (ca. 100 x 200m) excavated EB settlement with ca. 15 rooms and 50 stone circles on high ground on the *Wādi aš-Šeh*. Open cistern nearby.

¶ Courtesy of I. Beit-Arieh.

0478.03 P.g. 0491.7879

Name: *Šēḫ Muḥsin*, Ophir 1047.

Description: Excavated EB settlement (ca. 80 x 30m) with 10 circles and 5 rooms.

¶ Courtesy of I. Beit-Arieh.

0578.01 P.g. 0510.7894

Name: Ophir 1019.

Description: Remains: possibly EB.

¶ Courtesy of I. Beit-Arieh.

0578.02 P.g. 0520.7896

Name: Ophir 1018.

Description: Remains: possibly EB.

¶ Courtesy of I. Beit-Arieh.

0578.03 P.g. 0506.7851 E.g. 31° 9069.6632

Name: *Šēh Nabī Sāliḥ*, Roth 380.

Description: Very large (ca. 150 x 500m) excavated EB settlement with ca. 250 stone circles, enclosures and tumuli on high ground in *Wādi aš-Šēḫ*. Springs: 0520.7850; 0496.7847; also some Egyptian early dynastic pottery found.

¶ Rothenberg, Ha-Aretz 11, 1969, 30; idem, PEQ 102, 1970, 27; Beit-Arieh, Hadashot Archaeologiot 1973, 42; further, courtesy of I. Beit-Arieh and B. Rothenberg.

0578.04 P.g. 0516.7856

Name: Ophir 1030.

Description: EB settlement with 7 rooms and stone circles.

¶ Courtesy of I. Beit-Arieh.

0578.05 P.g. 0536.7853

Name: Ophir 1033.

Description: EB settlement in *Wādi Ramti* with ca. 10 rooms and stone circles.

¶ Courtesy of I. Beit-Arieh.

0578.06 P.g. 0542.7858

Name: Roth 589.

Description: Small Chalcolithic-EB I settlement with attached stone enclosures and some Nawami-like structures.

(0578.06)

¶ Courtesy of B. Rothenberg.

0578.07 P.g. 0540.7853

Name: Ophir 1034.

Description: EB settlement (ca. 35 x 20m) with 2 rooms and stone circle in *Wādi Ramti*.

¶ Courtesy of I. Beit-Arieh.

0578.08 P.g. 0575.7856

Name: Roth 587B.

Description: Small settlement (ca. 10 x 15m) with Nawami-like structure and Chalcolithic-EB I pottery and flints.

¶ Courtesy of B. Rothenberg.

0578.09 P.g. 0508.7841

Name: Ophir 1040.

Descrpption: Small settlement on both sides of wādi with stone enclosures, circles and tumuli with possibly EB Egyptian related pottery and flints.

¶ Courtesy of I. Beit-Arieh.

0578.10 P.g. 0588.7840

Name: Roth 596.

Description: Small settlement with attached stone structures and 1 tumulus near copper mines with possibly Chalcolithic-EB I or EB pottery and flints, as well as some Egyptian related Proto- or early dynastic pottery.

¶ Courtesy of B. Rothenberg.

0579.11 P.g. 0581.7831

Name: Roth 590, Ophir 1035.

Description: Excavated EB metallurgical site (ca. 70 x 40m).

¶ Courtesy of I. Beit-Arieh and B. Rothenberg.

0578.12 P.g. 0572.7807

Name: Ophir 1041.

Description: EB metallurgical site (ca. 100 x 60m).

¶ Courtesy of I. Beit-Arieh.

0578.13 P.g. 0591.7800

Name: Ophir 1036.

Description: Small settlement with rooms and stone circles near copper mines with EB flints.

¶ Courtesy of I. Beit-Arieh.

0678.01 P.g. 0614.7840

Name: Roth 594.

Description: Small settlement with a little EB pottery and flints.

¶ Courtesy of B. Rothenberg.

0678.02 P.g. 0606.7838

Name: Roth 600.

Description: Small settlement with stone circles, with possibly Chalcolithic-EB I or EB flints.

¶ Courtesy of B. Rothenberg.

0678.03 P.g. 0635.7835

Name: Roth 593.

Description: Large Chalcolithic-EB I settlement with Nawami-like structures.

¶ Courtesy of B. Rothenberg.

0678.04 P.g. 0610.7829 E.g. 31° 9165.6166

Name: Roth 381.

Description: Settlement with some Nawami-like structures with both Chalcolithic-EB I and EB pottery and flints.

¶ Rothenberg, Ha-Aretz 11, 1969, 32; further, courtesy of B. Rothenberg.

0678.05 P.g. 0638.7810

Name: Roth 601B.

Description: Small settlement with stone circles and Chalcolithic-EB I flints.

¶ Courtesy of B. Rothenberg.

0878.01 P.g. 0840.7868

Name: Roth 383.

Description: Chalcolithic-EB I remains.

¶ Rothenberg, Ha-Aretz 11, 1969, Pl.IV.

0878.02 P.g. 0856.7869

Name: Roth 384.

Description: Remains with possibly Chalcolithic-EB I pottery and flints.

¶ Rothenberg, Ha-Aretz 11, 1969, Pl.IV; further, courtesy of B. Rothenberg.

0878.03 P.g. 0893.7843

Name: Ophir 1003.

Description: Possibly Chalcolithic-EB I remains.

¶ Courtesy of I. Beit-Arieh.

0878.04 P.g. 0895.7840

Name: Ophir 1004.

Description: Possibly Chalcolithic-EB I remains.

¶ Courtesy of I. Beit-Arieh.

0978.01 P.g. 0902.7837

Name: Ophir 1002.

Description: Large Chalcolithic-EB I settlement (ca. 100 x 70m) with ca. 100 stone circles.

¶ Courtesy of I. Beit-Arieh.

0978.02 P.g. 0918.7820

Name: Ophir 1005.

Description: Settlement (ca. 80 x 50m) with possibly Chalcolithic-EB I remains.

¶ Courtesy of I. Beit-Arieh.

0978.03 P.g. 0920.7819

Name: Ophir 1006.

Description: Possibly Chalcolithic-EB I remains.

¶ Courtesy of I. Beit-Arieh.

0978.04 P.g. 0924.7817

Name: Ophir 1008.

Description: Chalcolithic-EB I settlement with ca. 12 rooms and stone circles.

¶ Courtesy of I. Beit-Arieh.

0978.05 P.g. 0920.7816

Name: Ophir 1007.

Description: Possibly Chalcolithic-EB I remains.

¶ Courtesy of I. Beit-Arieh.

0978.06 P.g. 0930.7808

Name: Ophir 1009.

Description: Chalcolithic-EB I remains.

¶ Courtesy of I. Beit-Arieh.

0177.01 P.g. 011.779 E.g. 31° 8663.6558

Name: Roth 480.

Description: Chalcolithic-EB I settlement with several stone circles and 1 large tumulus.

¶ Courtesy of B. Rothenberg.

0277.01

0277.01 P.g. 021.779 E.g. 31° 8670.6566

Name: Roth 481A.

Description: Large Chalcolithic-EB I flint workshop.

¶ Courtesy of B. Rothenberg.

0676.01 P.g. 0641.7686

Name: Roth 454.

Description: Chalcolithic-EB I metallurgical site with many tumuli and cist tombs.

¶ Courtesy of B. Rothenberg.

0776.01 P.g. 0794.7686

Name: Roth 453.

Description: Chalcolithic-EB I metallurgical site.

¶ Courtesy of B. Rothenberg.

0876.01 P.g. 0883.7641

Name: Roth 450.

Description: Small Chalcolithic-EB I settlement with some Nawami-like structures.

¶ Courtesy of B. Rothenberg.

1076.01 P.g. 1003-8.7683

Name: Roth 385.

Description: Chalcolithic-EB I copper mine.

¶ Rothenberg, Ha-Aretz 11, 1969, 32.

0775.01 P.g. 0703.7502

Name: Roth 426.

Description: Several tumuli on terrace with possibly Chalcolithic-EB I or EB II flints.

(0775.01)

¶ Courtesy of B. Rothenberg.

0873.01 P.g. 0879.7358

Name: Roth 422.

Description: Small settlement with stone structures near modern mine with possibly Chalcolithic-EB I or EB pottery and flints.

¶ Courtesy of B. Rothenberg.

0672.01 P.g. 0699.7251

Name: Roth 445.

Description: Tumuli with some possibly Chalcolithic-EB I pottery.

¶ Courtesy of B. Rothenberg.

0771.01 P.g. 0753.7180

Name: Roth 438.

Description: Small Chalcolithic-EB I settlement (ca. 40 x 30m) with a group of 6 stone circles.

¶ Courtesy of B. Rothenberg.

0771.02 P.g. 0774.7167

Name: Roth 437A.

Description: Chalcolithic-EB I settlement.

¶ Courtesy of B. Rothenberg.

0771.03 P.g. 0774.7163

Name: Roth 437.

Description: Chalcolithic-EB I settlement with 4 stone circles.

¶ Courtesy of B. Rothenberg.

INDEX OF ARABIC NAMES

ʿAin ʿAbda
1203.33.34
1202.16.17.26

Wādi ʿAbda
1202.23.24.25.26.34.36
.37.38.39.40.41.42
.43.44.45.46.47.48
.52.54.62.63.64.65
.66.67.68.76.77
1101.13.14.15.17
1201.17.18

Wādi Abu Rūta̱
1002.03

Wādi Abu Sayyāl
0501.02.03

Rās al-Abyaḍ
1102.01.02.03.04.05.06
.07.08.09.10.11.12
.13.14

Wādi al-Abyaḍ
1202.07.08.09.10.11.12
.19.22.50
0801.01

Ǧ. Umm ʿAdawī
0672.01

Wādi al-Aǧram
1199.01.02
1299.01

Wādi Aǧramīya
1297.02

ʿAin al-Aḥmad
0983.01

Ǧ. al-ʿAin
0900.02.04.05.09

Wādi ʿAin
0900.01.03.04.08

Al-ʿAina
2204.01

Gulf of ʿAqaba (al-ʿAqaba)
1488.04

Wādi al-ʿAraba
1905.01
1804.04
1803.01
1592.03.06
1491.06.07.08.09.10.12.14
1490.01
1590.01.02
1488.04

Wādi ʿArʿara
1405.01.02
1505.01.02.03.04

Wādi ʿArāǧīn
1303.10.11.12.14.15.20
.21.22.23.24.25.27
.28.30.31.32.35.36

Wādi al-ʿAsalī
1000.04

Wādi al-ʿAuǧāʾ
0902.01.02.03.04.05.06
.07.09.10.11.12.13
1002.07.08.15

Wādi al-ʿAusaǧī
1204.01

Wādi al-Baqara
1203.32

Wādi al-Baqqār
1203.04.05
1305.01.02.03.06.07.08
.09.13

Al-Baqqār
1203.10

Ǧ. Barakāt
0672.01

Wādi Bayāḍ
9887.01

Wādi Birēn
0901.01.02.03

Bīr al-Biyār
0682.01

Wādi Umm Burēriq
1198.01.03

ʿAin ad-Dēl
1592.03.06

Wādi ad-Dēl
1592.02

ʿAin ad-Dēsa
9591.01

Ǧ. aḏ-Ḏirāʿ
2004.01

Ǧ. Ergab Esdud
1202.51.52.53.62.63.64
.65.66

Wādi aš-Šeqer
1900.01

Wādi Faiʾ
1504.01.02

Fēnān
1900.01

Ǧazīrat Firʿaun
1387.01

Fuqēqis
2105.01

ʿAin Ǧāba
2104.02

Wādi Abū Ǧaṯaba
1593.01

Wādi al-Ġēdara
9794.01.02.03.04.06.07
.08.09.10

Wādi Umm Ǧidla
9788.02

Ġōr aṣ-Ṣāfi
1905.01

Ḫ. Umm Ǧrfn
1304.01

Wādi al-Ǧurf
1404.03.04.05.06.08.09
.10
1303.04.05.16.17.20

Wādi al-Ġuwēr
1900.01

Wādi al-Ḥafīr
1002.02.04.05.06.09.10
.11.12.13
1001.02.03
1000.06.08

Ǧ. Halāl
0501.03.05.06.07.08.09

Wādi Ḥalēqūm
1203.21.22.23.24.27.28
.29.30.31
1303.18.19.26.33.34.37
.38.39.42

Ǧ. Ḫarūf
1098.01.02

Rās Ḫarūf
1099.02.04

Wādi Ḫarūf
1099.02

Wādi Umm Ḫarūba
1203.04.05.16.17.18.19
.20

Wādi Umm Hāšim
0900.08.12.14.15.16
1000.13

Wādi Ḥaṯīra
1404.07.09.10

Wādi al-Ḫawwā
1300.01.02.04

Wādi Ḫudēra
2105.01

Tall al-Ḫulēfa
1488.04

Rās al-Ḫurāša
1099.05.06
1199.07.08.09.10.11.14
.15.19

Wādi Ḫurāša
1001.01.05.06.07
1000.01.03.06.08
1099.03
1199.03.04.05.06

Wādi al-Huwar
1000.12

Wādi Imsura
1203.09

Wādi Isdarīya
1003.01.02

ʿAin Umm Kaʿb
1302.09

Wādi Umm Kaʿb
1302.09

Katīb al-Qals
9607.01

Kurnub
1504.04

Wādi Lusṣān
1099.05.06

Wādi Maʿātiq
0889.01

Wādi al-Maharug
1303.43
1302.03

Ǧ. Mahawīya
1202.20.21.22.23.24

ʿAin Tisār al-Māliḥ
9691.01

Wādi Mandar
0672.01

Wādi Maqraʿa
1097.01

Wādi al-Marra
1203.34
1202.03
1302.01.02.03.05.06.07
.08

Wādi al-Mašāš
0501.01

Al-Maṭrada
1101.01.02.03.04.06.07
.08.09.10.11.12
1201.01.02.05

Wādi al-Maṭrada
1202.69.70.71.72.73.74
1101.03.04.05.08
1201.01.02.03.04.05.06
.07.08.09.10.11.12
.13.14.15.16

Wādi al-Māyēn
1197.01

Wādi el Migrin
1103.02

Wādi al-Milḥān
1491.06

Wādi Mirzaba
1501.01

Wādi Muʿaṯiq
0889.01.05

Al-Mudawwara
2105.02

ʿAin Muġāra
1098.04.05
1097.01

Wādi Muʿēḏir
1198.02
1297.01

Šēḫ Muḥsin
0478.02.03

Wādi al-Munēʿīya
1490.02.06.08.11.13.17

Wādi al-Muqēr
2105.02

ʿAin Murēfiq
1202.26

Wādi Mūsā
1997.01

Wādi al-Mušāš
1405.01.02

Wādi Mušēša aš-Šarqīya
1301.02.03

Ḫ. al-Mušimmīn
2103.01

Muwēliḥ
0801.01

Wādi Muwēliḥ
0801.01.02

Šēḫ Nabī Sāliḥ
0578.03

Ǧ. an-Nafḫ
1202.75.76.77

Wādi an-Nafḫ
1201.19.20
1301.01
1200.01.02.03.04.05.06
.07.08

Naqb al-Ġārib
1303.41

Bīr Naṣb
9982.01.02

ʿAin Niǧil
2099.01

Wādi Niǧil
2099.01

Wādi an-Namra
1490.19

ʿAin Abū al-Nutēqina
0085.01

Petra
1997.01

Bīr al-Qals
9607.01

Wādi Qaṣā
1298.03

Wādi Qatun
1101.09.10.16.17

Wādi Qaṭērī
1003.03
1002.01

Wādi Qisil
9887.04

ʿAin al-Qudērāt
0900.02.05.06.09.10.10A
.11.13.15

Wādi al-Qudērāt
0900.06.07
1000.04.09.10.11

ʿAin Qudēs
0900.17.18
1000.09
1099.01

Wādi Qudēs
1099.01

Wādi Qulēṭa
1593.01

ʿAin Quṣēma
0801.02
0900.01.03

Ǧ. Raḫama
1304.04

Tall Raḫama
1304.04

Wādi Raḫama
1304.01.02
1404.01.02

Ḫ. Raḫama
1404.04

Wādi Raintīya
1202.75

Rās ar-Ramān
1199.16.17.18.19

Wādi Ramān
1401.01
1299.02

Wādi Ramti
0578.05.07

ʿAin ar-Ratama
9591.01

Naqb Umm Ratama
1202.27.28.29.30.31.32
.33.34.35

Ruǧm al-Balawī
1505.08.09.10

Ruǧm Hadīd
1590.02

Wādi Rusēsīya
1002.13.14.16.17

Wādi Ṣabḥa
0801.02

Aṣ-Ṣāfi
1904.01

Wādi Umm Ṣāliḥ
1298.01

Wādi aš-Šallāla
9887.01

Sarābīt al-Ḫādim
9982.04

Ḫ. aṣ-Ṣerâreh
2104.01

Wādi Umm Sarānīq
0501.03.04.06.07.08

Wādi aš-Šēḫ
0279.02
0479.05
0478.01.02
0578.03

Wādi as-Sīr
1504.08.09

Ḫ. Umm aṣ-Ṣudēra
2104.02

ʿAin Sudr
9691.01

Wādi as-Sudr
9591.01
9691.01

Bīr aṭ-Ṭamad
0889.05

Wādi aṭ-Ṭamad
0889.05

Wādi Theigat el ʿAmirin
1203.01.02.06.07.08.09
.11.12
1202.01.02.04.05.06.08
.13.14.15.18.20

Wādi Ṭurēfa
9887.04

Wādi al-Ubara
1397.01

Bīr ʿUdēd
1297.05

Wādi al-ʿUdēd
1298.02
1297.03

Wādi al-ʿUqfī
1491.06

Wādi ʿUslūǧ
1205.01
1204.02

Wādi ʿUzēz
1001.04

Wādi Yaman
1504.10

ʿAin Yarqa
0086.01

Wādi Yerga
1504.03.04.05.06.07

Wādi Zafra
2103.01

Wādi az-Zayyātīn
1103.03.04

Az-Zūfāʾ
1404.02

INDEX OF HEBREW NAMES

Naḥal Bəroqå
1198.01.03

Naḥal Bəśor
1203.06.09.11.12.13.15
1202.01.02.04.05.06.08
.13.14.15.18.20

Har Boqer
1203.25.26

Ḥ. Naḥal Boqer
1203.20

Naḥal Boqer
1203.04.05.16.17.18.19
.20
1303.01.02.03.06.07.08
.09.13

Råmat Boqer
1203.10

Naḥal Daro<u>k</u>
1303.43
1302.03

Borot Dimonå
1505.05

Dimonå
1505.06.07.08.09.10

Naḥal ᵓEfᶜe
1504.01.02

ᵓEᶦlat
1388.07
1488.03

Gulf of ᵓElat
1488.04

Har ᵓEldåd
1202.75.76.77

Naḥal ᵓElonim
1099.05.06

Naḥal ᵓElot
1199.03.04.05.06

Har ᶜĔzuz
1101.04

Naḥal ᶜĔzuz
0902.01.02.04.05.06
1002.07.08.15
1001.04

Ha-Makteš Ha-Gådol
1404.07.09.10

Naḥal Gəråfon
1301.02.03

Naḥal Gešur
1297.03

Har Ḥårif
1099.02.04
1098.01.02

Naḥal Ḥårif
1099.02

Naḥal Håroᶜå
1203.21.22.23.24.27.28
.29.30.31
1303.18.19.26.33.34.37
.38.39.42

Naḥal Håṣåṣ
1303.30.31.35.36

Naḥal Ḥåsni
1000.06.08

Naḥal Ḥawwå
1300.01.02.04

Naḥal Bəẹr Ḥayil
1203.04.05.09

Naḥal Ḥoršȧ
1101.01.05.07
1000.06.08
1099.03

Bəẹr Karkom
1297.05

Naḥal Karkom
1297.03
1397.01

Naḥal Laʿănȧ
1101.09.10.16.17

Har Lȧvȧn
1102.01.02.03.04.05.06
.07.08.09.10.11.12
.13.14

ʿEn Maʿărif
1202.26

Naḥal Maḥmȧl
1401.01

Ḥ. Mamšit
1504.04

Naḥal Mamšit
1504.03.04.05.06.07

Naḥal Marzẹvȧ
1501.01

Naḥal Mašʾabim
1304.01

Naḥal Maʿsẹr
1297.01

Naḥal Maṭrẹd
1202.69.70.71.72.73.74
1101.03.04.05.08
1201.01.02.03.04.05.06
.07.08.09.10.11.12
.13.14.15.16.17

Rȧmat Maṭrẹd
1101.01.02.03.04.06.07
.08.09.10.11.12
1201.01.02.05

ʿEn Ha-Məʿȧrȧ
1098.04.05
1097.01

Naḥal Məȧzẹr
1198.02

Naḥal Məśurȧ
1103.03.04

Naḥal Meteq
1491.06

Har Miḥyȧ
1202.20.21.22.23.24

Rogem Miqrȧ
1590.02

Naḥal Mirbȧṣ
1505.02.03.04

Naḥal Mitgȧn
1001.05.06.07
1000.01.03.06

Ḥ. Nȧzir
1405.02

Naḥal Nəḥuštȧn
1490.02.06.08.11.13.17

Naḥal Nimrȧ
1490.19

Naḥal Niṣȧnȧ
1002.02.04.05.06.09.10
.11.12.13
1001.02.03
1199.01.02
1299.01

Bəẹr Orȧ
1490.20

Naḥal Orȧ
1490.20.21.22

Naḥal ᶜOrẹd
1298.01

Naḥal Qȧdẹš Barnẹ ᶜa
1000.09.10.11

Naḥal Qəṣi ᶜa
1298.03

Biqᶜat Qəṭurȧ
1593.01

Naḥal Qȯrḥȧ
1103.02

Naḥal Rȧḥȧm
1590.02

ᶜEn Rȧḥẹl
1600.01

Har Rȧmon
1199.16.17.18.19.20

Makteš Rȧmon
1299.02

Givᶜat Refed
1404.02

Naḥal Refed
1404.01.02.03
1504.08.09

Har Rəḥabᶜȧm
1388.08

Naḥal Rəḥabᶜȧm
1388.08

Bəẹr Rəsisim
1002.16

Naḥal Rəsisim
1002.13.14.16.17

Har Rətȧmim
1202.27.28.29.30.32.33
.34.35

Naḥal Rətȧmim
1202.34.36.38.39.40.41
.42.43.44.45.46.47
.48

Naḥal Rȧviv
1003.03
1002.02

Naḥal Rəvivim
1205.01
1204.02
1304.01.02
1303.04.05.16.17

Har Romẹm
1099.05.06
1199.07.08.09.10.11.14
.15.19

Naḥal Rut
1002.03

Naḥal Šəḥoret
1489.04

Naḥal Šəlomo
1388.07

Naḥal Seḵer
1405.01.02

Naḥal Sidrā
1003.01.02

Naḥal Ṣin
1203.34
1202.03.75.76.77
1302.01.02.03.05.06.07
.08
1201.19.20
1301.01
1200.01.02.03.04.05.06
.07.08

Śədẹ Ṣin
1303.41
1302.01.02

Naḥal Ṣippŏrim
1203.32
1202.07.08.09.10.11.12
.19.22.50

Biqʿat Šizāfon
1593.01

Naḥal Šuʿālim
1404.09.10

ʿẸn Tāmār
1804.03.04

Timnaʿ
1490.07

Ḥ. Timnaʿ
1491.20

Naḥal Timnaʿ
1491.07.08.09.10.11.12
.14.15.19.20.21.22.23
1490.01

Naḥal Yafruq
1297.02

Naḥal Yāmin
1504.10

Har Yəroḥām
1304.04

Naḥal Yəroḥām
1404.04.05

Tẹl Yəroḥām
1304.04

Naḥal Yitnān
1405.01.02

ʿẸn Yōṭvātā
1592.03.06

Naḥal Yōṭvātā
1592.02

Naḥal Zalzal
1203.01.02.07.08.14

SPECIAL INDEX

Glueck Sites

Glueck Sites

307	1404.07
310	1404.06
311	1505.09
311A	1505.10
311B	1505.08
329	0902.09
330	0902.04
330A	0902.05
330B	1002.08
331	1002.15
331A	0901.02
334	1002.09
337	0902.12
339	0901.03
340	0901.01
343	1001.04
345	1002.10
346	1001.01
349	1200.01
361A-G	1304.04
367	1002.02
369	1002.03
372	1003.02
373	1003.01
410	1101.16
421	1000.06
424	1000.09
436	1302.04
436A	1302.07

Glueck Sites

437	1302.08
439	1302.06
440	1302.05
441	1302.03
452	1501.01
471	1098.05
471A	1097.01
472	1199.13
473	1199.11
474	1099.06
475	1098.02
476	1099.02
477	1098.03
481A	1397.01
483	1297.01
484	1297.02
485	1297.03
485	1297.04
485	1297.05
493	1298.03
II 14	1900.01
II 221	2204.01
II 232	2103.01
III 87	2104.02
III 88	2104.01

Ophir (Beit-Arieh) Sites

1002	0978.01
1003	0878.03

Ophir (Beit-Arieh) Sites

1004	0878.04
1005	0978.02
1006	0978.03
1007	0978.05
1008	0978.04
1009	0978.06
1014	0579.12
1016	0579.05
1017	0579.06
1018	0578.02
1019	0578.01
1020	0579.10
1021	0579.11
1022	0579.09
1023	0579.08
1024	0579.07
1030	0578.04
1033	0578.05
1034	0578.07
1035	0578.11
1036	0578.13
1040	0578.09
1041	0578.12
1042	0479.05
1044	0478.01
1047	0478.03

Råmat Matred Sites

15	1300.03

Råmat Maṭred, Aharoni Sites

22	1200.03
24	1299.01
30	1199.11
31	1099.05
33	1199.03
37	1199.18
38	1199.12
39	1199.02
45	1300.02
110	1102.04
111	1102.05
112	1102.03
115	1201.01
127	1201.06
131	1101.03
132	1202.50
133	1201.11
134	1201.09
135	1101.05
137	1101.08
139	1202.69
150	1102.02
152	1202.70
154	1202.56
155	1202.58
157	1202.60
160	1201.05
161	1202.55
162	1202.72

Ramat Maṭred, Aharoni Sites	
163	1202.73
166	1101.15
167	1101.14
168	1201.18
171	1201.17
173	1201.13
174	1201.15
176	1102.09
177	1102.07
178	1102.08
181	1102.13
182	1102.12
183	1101.01
185	1101.06
186	1101.10

Rothenberg Sites	
2	1491.20
3	1491.24
9	1491.15
10	1490.14
12	1490.01
13	1491.22
14	1491.23
15	1491.21
18	1491.16
19	1491.17
21	1491.19
22	1491.18

Rothenberg Sites	
23	1491.11
24	1491.07
25	1491.08
26	1590.01
27	1590.02
28	1490.22
29	1490.15
30	1490.02
31	1593.01
31	1490.03
32	1489.02
33	1489.03
33A	1489.04
34	1490.06
35	1490.11
37	1490.19
39	1490.13
39A	1490.16
39B	1490.12
40	1488.03
42	1490.18
43	1387.01
44	1592.07
45	1592.05
46	1488.02
50B	1804.03
51	1803.01
53	1704.01
54	1704.02

Rothenberg Sites	
56	1804.01
56B	1800.01
57	1600.01
57A	1600.02
64	1490.23
66	1490.17
67	1804.04
67A	1804.04
81	1489.06
82	1488.02
86	1388.07
102	1000.02
103	1000.05
104	1000.09
108A	1000.07
109	1000.10
110	1000.08
119	1489.05
122	1489.07
131	1591.04
132	1390.04
133	1390.03
134	1390.02
139	1390.01
141	1391.03
143	1391.04
144	1389.01
146	1389.03
146A	1389.02

Rothenberg Sites	
153	1491.02
154	1391.05
166	1492.04
167	1492.03
167A	1492.03
168	1492.01
170	1493.05
171	1493.03
172	1493.02
177	1391.02
179	1391.01
185	1490.08
186	1491.09
188	1490.10
189	1591.06
190	1591.05
191	1491.03
193	1490.09
194	1490.05
195	1490.04
196	1490.05
198	1490.05
199	1490.05
200	1490.07
201	1591.02
202	1591.01
203	1592.09
205	1592.08
205A	1592.08

Rothenberg Sites		Rothenberg Sites	
205B	1592.08	321	1388.04
207	1591.03	322	1288.03
209	1592.01	323	1288.02
210	1491.12	324	1288.01
211	1491.13	328	1189.04
212	1491.14	329	1189.03
213	1592.04	330	1189.02
215	1488.05	331	1089.05
217	1388.08	332	1089.04
225	1389.04	333	1089.03
226	1491.01	334	1089.02
227	1491.04	336	0889.02
229	1491.05	337	0889.01
229A	1491.06	338	0889.04
231	1493.01	341	9691.01
232	1493.04	343	9591.01
233	1492.02	344	9983.03
234	1492.05	344A	9983.02
235	1492.06	348	9882.01
236	1492.07	349	9883.02
237	1592.02	349A	9883.01
239	1594.01	350	9982.02
306	0900.10A	351	9982.03
307	0997.01	352	9982.01
309	0995.01	354	9983.01
310	1388.03	355	9982.04
311	1388.05	357	9981.01
312	1388.06	359	9881.01
320	1388.01	360	9980.01

Rothenberg Sites

363	0080.01
364	9979.01
366	0179.02
367	0179.03
368	0179.01
369	0080.02
370	9879.02
371	9879.01
372	9980.02
373	0179.04
374	0279.01
375	0279.02
378	0479.03
379	0479.04
380	0578.03
381	0678.04
383	0878.01
384	0878.02
385	1076.01
388	0880.01
389	0880.02
391	0779.02
392	0879.01
393	1086.01
397	0981.01
398	1082.01
399	1083.01
413	1387.02
414	1386.01

Rothenberg Sites

418	1490.24
422	0873.01
426	0775.01
437	0771.03
437A	0771.02
438	0771.01
445	0672.01
450	0876.01
453	0776.01
454	0676.01
460	0479.02
461	0480.02
462	0480.03
465	0480.01
468	0379.01
469	0379.02
471	0479.01
472	0579.04
473	0579.02
474	0579.03
480	0177.01
481A	0277.01
491	0780.03
494	0780.02
495	0780.01
496	0779.01
499	0779.03
501	0579.01
502	0681.03

Rothenberg Sites	
503A-G	0681.06
504	0681.05
505	0681.04
506	0681.02
507	0782.03
509A	0882.01
510	0983.01
511	0982.01
511A	0982.02
513	0682.01
514	0683.09
515	0683.08
516	0683.07
517	0682.02
518	0682.03
519	0782.02
520	0782.01
521	0681.01
522A	0580.01
527	0181.01
531	0182.01
533	0082.01
535	0084.01
537	9786.01
540	9886.03
545	9986.02
546	9986.01
547	9987.01
549	9886.02

Rothenberg Sites	
550	9886.01
552	9887.05
554	9694.02
554A	9694.01
565	9493.02
567	9493.01
578	9495.01
579	9495.02
580	9696.01
581	9695.01
584	1388.02
587B	0578.08
589	0578.06
590	0578.11
593	0678.03
594	0678.01
596	0578.10
600	0678.02
601B	0678.05
618	1389.05
619	0990.01
620	0990.02
621	0889.03
624	0788.01
625	0788.02
629	0588.01
630	0587.01
631	0586.01
632	0586.02

Rothenberg Sites	
634	0586.03
635	0586.04
636	0685.01
637	0685.02
638	0685.03
639	0685.04
640	0684.01
642	0683.05
643	0683.06
644	0683.04
645	0683.03
646	0683.02
647	0683.01
649	1089.01
650	1189.01
651	1089.07
652	1089.06
657	1090.01
674	0499.01
676	9887.04
677	9887.01
678	9887.02
679	9888.01
684	9787.01
687	9788.04
688	9788.03
689	9788.02
691	9788.01
692	9887.03

Rothenberg Sites	
695	0086.01
696	0085.01
697	0085.02
699	0889.05

PERIODS

CHALCOLITHIC-EB I

0205.01.02

9604.01

1504.04

1202.04.05.06.

0499.01

9495.01.02

9695.01

9694.01

1493.01.02.03.04.05

1492.01.02.03.04.05.06.07

1592.01.02.04.07.08.09

9591.01

9691.01

1391.01.02.03.04.05

1491.01.02.03.04.05.06.
.14

1591.01.02.03.04.05.06

0990.01.02

1090.01

1390.01.02.03.04

1490.03.07.10.12.13.15
.16.18.24

0889.01.02.03.04

1089.01.02.03.04.05.06.07

1189.01.02.03.04

1389.01.02.03.04.05

1489.06.07

9788.01.02.03.04

9888.01

0588.01

0788.01.02

1288.02.03

1388.01.02.03.04.05.06

1488.02.05

9887.02.04.05

0587.01

1387.02

9786.01

Chalcolithic-EB I

9886.01.02

0086.01

0586.01.02.03.04

1086.01

1386.01

0085.01.02

0685.01.02.03.04

0084.01

0684.01

9883.01

9983.03

0683.01.02.03.04.05.06
.07.08.09

0983.01

1083.01

9882.01

9982.02.04

0182.01

0682.01.02.03

0782.01.02.03

0882.01

0982.01.02

1082.01

9881.01

0181.01

0681.01.02.03.04.05.06

0981.01

9980.01.02

0080.01.02

0480.01.02.03

Chalcolithic-EB I

0580.01

0780.01.02.03

0880.01.02

9879.01.02

9979.01

0179.01.02.03.04

0279.01.02

0379.01.02

0479.01.02.04

0579.01

0779.01.02.03

0879.01

0578.06.08.10

0678.02.03.04.05

0878.01.02.03.04

0978.01.02.03.04.05.06

0177.01

0277.01

0676.01

0776.01

0876.01

1076.01

0775.01

0873.01

0672.01

0771.01.02.03

EB

9607.01

EB

0105.01

0205.03.05

9604.02.03

1304.02

1404.04

1504.04

1804.04

2004.01

2104.02

2103.01

0902.06.08.13

1002.01

1202.04.05.06.21.23.24.34
.52.63

1301.02.03

1401.01

1997.01

9788.01.04

0588.01

9787.01

9887.04.05

1387.02

1386.01

0085.02

9883.02

0983.01

9982.04

0082.01

0182.01

0981.01

EB

0580.01

0780.01.02.03

0279.01.02

0379.01.02

0479.01.02.03.05

0579.05.06.07.08.09.10.11.12

0779.01.02.03

0879.01

0478.01.02.03

0578.01.02.03.04.05.07.09
.10.11.12.13

0678.01.02.04

0775.01

0873.01

EB IV/MB I

0105.01

0205.01.02

1205.01

1405.01.02

1505.01.02.03.04.05.06.07
.08.09.10

1905.01

2105.01.02

9604.02.03

1204.01.02

1304.01.03.04

1404.01.02.03.04.05.06.07
.08.09.10

1504.01.02.03.05.06.07.08.09.10

1804.02.04

EB IV/MB I

1904.01

2104.01.02

2204.01

1003.01.02.03

1103.01.02.03.04

1203.01.02.03.04.05.06.
.07.08.09.10.11.12
.13.14.15.16.17.18
.19.20.21.22.23.24
.25.26.27.28.29.30
.31.32.33.34.35.36

1303.01.02.03.04.05.06
.07.08.09.10.11.12
.13.14.15.16.17.18
.19.20.21.22.23.24
.25.26.27.28.29.30
.31.32.33.34.35.36
.37.38.39.40.41.42
.43

2103.01

0902.01.02.03.04.05.06
.07.08.09.10.11.12
.13

1002.01.02.03.04.05.06
.07.08.09.10.11.12
.13.14.15.16.17

1102.01.02.03.04.05.06
.07.08.09.10.11.12
.13.14

1202.01.02.03.04.05.06
.07.08.09.10.11.12
.13.14.15.16.17.18
.19.20.21.22.23.24
.25.26.27.28.29.30
.31.32.33.35.36.37
.38.39.40.41.42.43
.44.45.46.47.48.49
.50.51.53.54.55.56
.57.58.59.60.61.62
.64.65.66.67.68.69
.70.71.72.73.74.75
.76.77

1302.01.02.03.04.05.06
.07.08.09

EB IV/MB I

0501.01.02.03.04.05.06
.07.08.09

0801.01.02

0901.01.02.03

1001.01.02.03.04.05.06
.07

1101.01.02.03.04.05.06
.07.08.09.10.11.12
.13.14.15.16.17

1201.01.02.03.04.05.06
.07.08.09.10.11.12
.13.14.15.16.17.18
.19.20

1301.01

1501.01

0900.01.02.03.04.05.06
.07.08.09.10.10A
.11.12.13.14.15.16
.17.18

1000.01.03.04.06.08.09
.10.11.12.13

1200.01.02.03.04.05.06
.07.08

1300.01.02.03.04

1600.01

1800.01

1900.01

1099.01.02.03.04.05.06

1199.01.02.03.04.05.06
.07.08.09.10.11.12
.13.14.15.16.17.18
.19

1299.01.02

2099.01

1098.01.02.03.04.05

1198.01.02.03

EB IV/MB I

1298.01.02.03

0997.01

1097.01

1197.01

1297.01.02.03.04.05

1397.01

9696.01

9495.01.02

9695.01

9694.02

9794.01.02.03.04.05.06
.07.08.09.10

9493.01.02

1493.01.02.05.06

1492.03.04.08

9591.01

9691.01

1491.01.02.03.06.18.19

1490.03.20.21.22

0889.01.03.05

1389.05

1489.01.05

9788.03

9888.01

1488.03

9887.01.03.04.05

9987.01

1387.01

9786.01

9886.01.03

EB IV/MB I

9986.01.02

9983.03

9982.04

MB II

0205.01.04

9604.02.03

1504.07

2004.01

1489.01

9883.02

9982.01.02.03.04

9981.01

LB

9805.01.02

0105.01

9404.01.02.03

9504.01.02.03.04.05

1704.01.02

1804.01.03.04

1803.01

1000.02.05.07.09

1600.01.02

0995.01

1594.01

1493.01.02.03

1492.02.03.04.07

1592.03.05.06.07.08

LB

1391.05

1491.03.06.07.08.09.10
.11.12.13.14.15.16
.17.18.19.20.21.22
.23.24

1591.02

1490.01.02.04.05.06.07
.08.09.11.13.14.17
.19.23.24

1590.01.02

1089.02

1489.01.02.03.04

1288.01

1388.07.08

1488.01.02.04

1387.01

9983.01.02.03

9982.01.02.03.04

9979.01

0179.03.04

BIBLIOGRAPHY

Aharoni, Y., *The Land of Gerar*, IEJ 6, 1956, 26-32.

Aharoni, Y., *The Negeb of Judah*, IEJ 8, 1958, 26-38.

Aharoni, Y. et alii, *The Ancient Desert Agriculture of the Negev: III. Early Beginnings*, IEJ 8, 1958, 231-68.

Aharoni, Y. et alii, *The Ancient Desert Agriculture of the Negev: V. An Israelite Agricultural Settlement at Ramat Maṭred*, IEJ 10, 1960, 23-36; 97-111.

Aharoni Y., *The Negeb*, in Archaeology and Old Testament Study, ed. by D. W. Thomas (London 1967), 384-401.

Albright, W. F., *Abram the Hebrew, a New Archaeological Interpretation*, BASOR 163, 1961, 36-54.

Amiran, D. H. K., *Geomorphology of the Central Negev Highlands*, IEJ 1, 1951, 107-20.

Amiran, R. et alii, *The Interrelationship between Arad and Sites in Southern Sinai in the Early Bronze Age II*, IEJ 23, 1973, 193-97.

Ashbel, D., *On the Importance of Dew in Palestine*, JPOS 16, 1936, 316-21.

Ashbel, D., *Frequency and Distribution of Dew in Palestine*, The Geographical Review 39, 1949, 291-97.

Butzer, K. W. and Twindale, C. R., *Deserts in the Past*, in Arid Lands, ed. by E. S. Hills (London 1966).

Dothan, M., *An Archaeological Survey of Mt. Casius and its Vicinity*, EI 9, 1969, 47-59.

Efrat, E. and Orni, E., Geographie Israels (Jerusalem 1972).

Evenari, M. et alii, *Ancient Agriculture in the Negev*, Science 133, 1961, 979-96.

Evenari, M. et alii, The Negev (Cambridge, Massachusetts 1971).

Frank, F., *Aus der ʿAraba I*, ZDPV 57, 1934, 191-280.

Glueck, N., *Explorations in Eastern Palestine II*, AASOR 15, 1934-35.

Glueck,N., *Explorations in Eastern Palestine III*, AASOR 18-19, 1939.

Glueck, N., *Explorations in Western Palestine*, BASOR 131, 1953, 6-15.

Glueck, N., *Further Explorations in the Negeb*, BASOR 137, 1955, 10-22.

Glueck, N., *The Age of Abraham in the Negev*, BA 18, 1955, 2-9.

Glueck, N., *The Third Season of Explorations in the Negeb*, BASOR 138, 1955, 7-29.

Glueck, N., *The Fourth Season of Exploration in the Negeb*, BASOR 142, 1956, 17-35.

Glueck, N., *The Fifth Season of Exploration in the Negeb*, BASOR 145, 1957, 11-25.

Glueck, N., *The Sixth Season of Archaeological Exploration in the Negeb*, BASOR 149, 1958, 8-17.

Glueck, N., *The Seventh Sesson of Archaeological Exploration in the Negeb*, BASOR 152, 1958, 18-38.

Glueck, N., Rivers in the Desert (New Haven 1959).

Glueck, N., *An Aerial Reconnaissance of the Negev*, BASOR 155, 1959, 2-13.

Glueck, N., *The Negev*, BA 22, 1959, 82-97.

Glueck, N., *Archaeological Exploration of the Negeb in 1959*, BASOR 159, 1960, 3-14.

Glueck, N., *Further Exploration in the Negev*, BASOR 179, 1965, 6-29.

Hills, E. S., Arid Lands (London 1966).

Karmon, Y., Israel: A Regional Geography (London 1970).

Kedar, Y., *Ancient Agriculture in the Negev*, IEJ 7, 1957, 178-89.

Kedar, Y., *Water and Soil from the Desert: Some Ancient Agricultural Achievements in the Central Negev*, Geographical Journal 123, 1957, 179-87.

Kirk, G. E., *The Negev, or Southern Desert of Palestine*, PEQ 73, 1941, 57-71.

Kochavi, M., *The Excavation at Tel Yeruham*, BIES 27, 1963, 284-92.

Kochavi, M., The Settlement of the Negev in the MB I Age (Hebrew Univ. Diss., 1967).

Kochavi, M., *The Middle Bronze Age I (The Intermediate Bronze Age) in Eretz-Israel*, Qadmoniot 2, 1969, 38-44.

Lewis, N., *New Light on the Negev in Ancient Times*, PEQ 80, 1948, 102-30.

Margovsky, I., Hadashot Archaeologiot 28-29, 1969, 43-47.

Margovsky, I., *Notes and News*, IEJ 21, 1971, 236.

Margovsky, I., *Three Temples in Northern Sinai*, Qadmoniot 4, 1971, 18-20.

Marx, E., Bedouin of the Negev (Manchester 1967).

Mayerson, P., The Ancient Agricultural Regime of Nessana and the Central Negeb (London 1960).

Mayerson, P., *A Note on the Demography and Land Use in the Ancient Negev*, BASOR 185, 1967, 39-43.

Miroschedji, P. R. de, L'Époque Pré-Urbaine en Palestine, CRB 13 (Paris 1971).

Murray, G. W., *Water from the Desert: Some Ancient Egyptian Achievements*, Geographical Journal 121, 1955, 171-81.

Oren, E., *The Overland Route Between Egypt and Canaan in the Early Bronze Age*, IEJ 23, 1973, 198-205.

Orni, E. and Efrat, E., Geographie Israels (Jerusalem 1972).

Robinson, D. M., *Syria and Palestine*, AJA 39, 1935, 120f.

Rothenberg, B., God's Wilderness (London 1961).

Rothenberg, B., *Anicent Copper Industries in the Western Arabah*, PEQ 94, 1962, 5-71.

Rothenberg, B., *König Salomons Hafen im Roten Meer neu entdeckt*, Das Heilige Land 95, 1965, 19-28.

Rothenberg, B., *The Chalcolithic Copper Industry at Timna*, Museum Ha-Aretz Bulletin 8, 1966, 86-93.

Rothenberg, B., *Excavations in the Early Iron Age Copper Industries at Timna*, ZDPV 82, 1966, 125-35.

Rothenberg, B., *Excavations at Timna, 1964-1966*, Museum Ha-Aretz Bulletin 9, 1967, 53-70.

Rothenberg, B., Sfunot Negev (Negev: Archaeology in the Negev and the Arabah) Ramat Gan, 1967.

Rothenberg, B., *An Archaeological Survey of the Eloth District and the Southernmost Negev*, Museum Ha-Aretz Bulletin 10, 1968, 25-35.

Rothenberg, B., *An Archaeological Survey of South Sinai*, Museum Ha-Aretz Bulletin 11, 1969, 22-38.

Rothenberg, B., *An Archaeological Survey of South Sinai*, PEQ 102, 1970, 4-44.

Rothenberg, B., *An Egyptian Temple of Hathor Discovered in the Southern Arabah*, Museum Ha-Aretz Bulletin 12, 1970, 28-35.

Rothenberg, B., *Sinai Explorations 1967-1972*, Museum Ha-Aretz Bulletin 14, 1972, 31-45.

Rothenberg, B., Timna (London 1972).

Shanon, L. et alii, *Rainfall Patterns in the Central Negev Desert*, IEJ 17, 1967, 163-84.

Thompson, Th. L., The Historicity of the Patriarchal Narratives, BZAW 133 (Berlin 1974).

Thompson, Th. L., *Observations on the Bronze Age in Jordan*, ADAJ 1974, in press.

Thompson, Th. L., *Corrections to the Coordinates of Glueck's Negev Surveys*, ZDPV 91, 1975, in press.

Weippert, M., *Archäologisches Jahresbericht*, ZDPV 80, 1964, 150-93.

Whyte, R. O., *The Use of Arid and Semi-Arid Land*, in Arid Lands, ed. by E. S. Hills (London 1966), 312f.

Zohary, D., *Notes on Ancient Agriculture in the Central Negev*, IEJ 4, 1954, 17-25.